# DIFFERENT DAUGHTERS

5/98

Dear Mamos,

In honor of a

~ full of surprises ..

Mother's Day.

I love you.

Ariel

Also by Louise Rafkin

*Martial Arts: Mastering the Self*

*Streetsmarts: A Personal Safety Guide for Women*

*Queer and Pleasant Danger: Writing Out My Life*

*Different Mothers: Sons and Daughters of Lesbians Talk About Their Lives*

*Unholy Alliances: New Women's Fiction*

# Different Daughters

## A BOOK BY
## MOTHERS OF LESBIANS

### SECOND EDITION
*Revised & Expanded*

### EDITED BY
### LOUISE RAFKIN

Published in the United States by Cleis Press Inc., P.O. Box 8933, Pittsburgh, Pennsylvania 15221, and P.O. Box 14684, San Francisco, California 94114.

Cover illustration: Pacha Wasiolek
Book design and production: Pete Ivey
Cleis logo art: Juana Alicia

Printed in the United States.
Second Edition.
10 9 8 7 6 5 4 3 2 1

*Library of Congress Cataloging-in-Publication Data*

Different Daughters / edited by Louise Rafkin. -- 2nd ed.
    p.  cm.
    "April 1996"
    ISBN 1-57344-051-5 (cloth). -- ISBN 1-57344-050-7 (pbk.)
    1. Lesbians--United States--Family relationships--Case studies.
2. Mothers and daughters--United States--Case studies. 3. Parents of gays--United States--Case studies. I. Rafkin, Louise, 1958–
HQ75.6.U5D54  1996
306.874'3--dc20                    96-5354
                                      CIP

For Rhoda and Ruth

In memory of Ann Dawson

# Contents

## ACKNOWLEDGMENTS

My heartfelt appreciation goes to the hundreds of women, both mothers and daughters, who came out and shared their stories at bookstores and community centers across the country after the publication of the first edition of this book. Thanks to all those in the media who rallied for *Different Daughters*, especially the producers who tooks risks with this subject material long before lesbianism was a popular topic on daytime TV. I would also like to thank Bárbara Selfridge, honorary lesbian, for "spousal support" at my *Geraldo!* appearances.

# Introduction to the Second Edition:
## Still Different After All These Years

Ten years ago when I started the project which became the first edition of *Different Daughters*, I had no idea the impact my innocently conceived idea would have on the lives of so many women. I was a young, newly out lesbian, with a generally agreeable mom who was isolated in a fairly small conservative community. I wanted both for her to connect with other mothers dealing with similar issues and to get an idea of what my life was all about.

At that time, the world was far less accepting of sexual minorities; the word *lesbian* was rarely mentioned in public. Lesbian characters had not yet been featured on evening sitcoms, and MTV she-roes were hardly outspokenly gay. k.d. lang was a name bantered around our community, but she had yet to pose with a supermodel on one of the country's trendiest magazines. No one would have dreamed that the words *Lesbian Chic* could sidle up together, yet alone be emblazoned across the cover of *Newsweek* magazine. Out lesbian politicians were scarce, and the idea of one being a member of the President's cabinet was unimaginable.

Much has changed for lesbians during the past decade, and I for one find myself living a happier, more open life. Though violence towards gays and lesbians has risen, and full legal rights for homosexuals seem a glimmer on the horizon of the twenty-first century, on a day-to-day basis I hardly realize that I am part of a feared and scorned sexual minority. My family has always been fairly open to who I am, though over the years I have put them through quite a number of hoops. After some prodding, they now inquire about "personal issues," like my lovers, and, on occasion, they will champion gay rights and challenge homophobia.

But such acceptance hasn't been quite as smooth for other women, despite our new status as pop cultural icons. With twenty-five thousand copies of the first edition of *Different Daughters* in circulation, over the years I have received a constant stream of letters from both mothers and daughters spilling the details of the difficult process of loving across differences and despite judgments. The letters vary: from missives by grateful daughters telling how *Different Daughters* helped them to reconnect with their mothers, to secretive notes from guilty and grief-stricken mothers asking if we could talk confidentially. There have been hopeful letters from mothers thanking me for the book, as well as bitter letters from those who could not budge from feeling anger and disappointment.

All of this correspondence I have read with awe: I do not underestimate the importance of us finding acceptance within our families of origin. Running the risk of sounding like a Hallmark card or a Top Forty song: I believe in the power of love, to heal, to support us in this complicated and sometimes hostile world. I believe that prejudice and hate are overcome on a personal level, one relationship at a time. I also believe that many of the social and political problems we as gays and lesbians face could be better solved if we forged a wider support base, created coalitions that began in the opened arms of families and friends.

The percentage of college students who believe that homosexuality should be outlawed has dropped from fifty-seven percent in 1987, to an all-time low of thirty-four percent in 1995. But this is still far too high a figure to support such an outdated notion. It pains and angers me to hear the stories of the parents who have disowned their children. And these stories abound. I want to shake the disapproving parents and ask them, "What do you think parenting is? Cloning? Did you expect your children to grow up to think like you? Be like you?"

My experience with a wide range of families, as well as my

own relationship with my mother, has brought me to a new understanding of family dynamics around queerness. Most importantly, I came to understand that lesbianism is not always the big chasm in family relationships, but often a catalyst for difficulties in relationships that were already quite rocky or unresolved. Psychologists call this phenomenon the "presenting problem," meaning that although lesbianism is often the named reason why parent and children aren't getting along, under scrutiny, this is not always the real reason.

Once, at the Parents and Friends of Lesbians and Gays national conference in Chicago, I actually heard a mother complain about lesbian potlucks. "What is it about lesbians and potlucks?" she asked, her face quite full of pain. She was dressed immaculately, pearls and a gray cashmere suit. "Why can't she give a dinner party like everyone else?" I assured her there were lesbians who gave dinner parties, and straight people who held potlucks, but I don't think I fully convinced her. I saw her at the break bending the sympathetic ear of another finely dressed woman. Their conversation was about *futons*. "Yes! They sleep right on the floor!" the other exclaimed. The problem was obvious to me: this woman's class background was fueling her resentment of her daughter's "lifestyle." "*Everyone* in Japan sleeps on the floor," I quipped as I walked past.

But mothers are not the only ones to target sexuality for all their daughters' foibles. (Not that a futon on the floor is a foible—don't get me wrong!) One recently-out lesbian complained to me that her parents were uninterested in her female lover. "Were they interested in the men you dated before you came out?" I asked. "Hmm…" she admitted. "Not really."

And the oft-heard: "My mother hates what I wear." Really, isn't this a given? Can we really pin this on being lesbian? Even my straight friends say their mothers don't approve of how they dress. Aren't parental schisms common to all mother-daughter relationships? The queer quotient is often used to further already entrenched family dynamics.

None of this is easy. It's easier to blame everything on homophobia than to dive head first into deeper waters. Better to dig in your heels at the edge of the pit than to plunge right into the muck. Who wants to sort through that messy stuff, especially with your parents? But, after watching scores of daughters unravel their issues with their parents, I recommend trying to unpack the issue of lesbianism apart from whatever else is going on in the family.

At the most basic level, parenting involves a commitment to unconditional loving, though, sadly, parents often try to control their offspring by withdrawing their love. I received one especially heartfelt letter from a woman who sent *Different Daughters* to her folks, only to find it returned to her mailbox. The words "You are no longer our daughter" were scrawled across the front of the package. I hope that one day these hardened hearts will break, and in the breaking, break open. However, there are times I just want to rant and scream. Get over it and get on with it, I hear myself saying. Let your kids be themselves and move on to the important work of loving, supporting, and becoming friends with each other.

In hindsight, I can see that *Different Daughters* was crucial to my own journey towards familial acceptance. It was simple: I wanted my mother to love and accept me and I started from the top addressing what I thought was the most difficult block to that goal. Now I see my lesbianism more as a part of my life, part of the package of who I am and why my mother and I get along, and only sometimes, why we don't. It hasn't always been an easy road to full acceptance, yet through our struggles we have grown to love each other more deeply and, most importantly, really know each other. I am forever grateful to her for her bravery and for simply sticking it out and doing the work of changing.

\*    \*    \*

Over the past ten years, this book has served a wide range of people of many backgrounds, in several countries. I have appeared on local and nationwide TV programs with my mother. (Once, right before airtime, she and I had a huge fight. Nevertheless we trooped forward, showing the world that mothers and lesbian daughters can actually get along!) I have facilitated discussions at nearly sixty bookstores and community centers across the country, giving the chance to both mothers and daughters to talk about their issues and fears. In addition to learning a lot about parenting and about being a daughter, I have watched the most unaccepting mothers move towards acceptance. I have seen the most judgmental daughters come to understand their mothers' predicaments.

Fran Salen, who wrote under a pseudonym in the first edition of this book, was so wrought over her husband's unacceptance of their two lesbian daughters that she solicited help at one of our bookstore events. "What can I do?" she asked the audience of over a hundred lesbians. "My husband says I can't tell anyone. I don't feel like I am in the closet, I feel like I am in a locked trunk!" Several years later, I spotted this proud Jewish mother marching down Market Street as part of a San Francisco Gay Pride parade—flanked by her husband! Both had grown tremendously in a short span of time. The Salens' story is proof enough for me that even the most entrenched people are capable of great change.

For this edition, I specifically sought out mothers of younger lesbians. Despite the high rate of suicide among teenaged gay and lesbians, I erroneously thought it might be easier to come out to one's parents in these more liberal times. After all, the parents of these kids were raised in the sixties and often are not much older than I. Unfortunately, I was wrong. Even in the gay nineties, it is still hard to weave through the maze of parental expectations and disappointments. Illustrating how the stigma of having a lesbian daughter still persists, several of the new and about half of the original contributors to this book have chosen not to use their real names to identify their stories.

This time I have also included the mother of two bisexual women, and the brave testimony of a mother whose lesbian daughter is in the process of redefining her gender. Life is no longer quilted from black or white; shades of gray give the fabric of our experience depth and perspective.

I hope someday there will no longer be a need for this book, until that time, I am happy that my optimistically undertaken, youthful project continues to help those seeking comfort and understanding.

Louise Rafkin

*Truro, Massachusetts*
*January 1996*

FRAN HARRIS

# A Merry-Go-Round

We sat around the dinner table drinking coffee, reminiscing, enjoying
being together for the first time in
over a year, my husband, my son and
my two daughters. We had about two
hours before we would have to drive
Laurie to the airport. And then our
youngest daughter, Joyce, dropped the
bomb:

"I have something to tell you," she
said. "It's not easy to tell, but I feel
that I have to say it now."

We all began to guess, laughingly
at first, but then we saw how serious
she looked and how her eyes filled up
with tears. It was no longer a joke. To
each of our guesses Joyce said, "No,
it's not that." Then my husband said
jokingly, "You're a lesbian, too."
When Joyce said, "That's it," my hus-
band, son and I were speechless, in a state of shock.

We had grown accustomed to the fact that our oldest
daughter, Laurie, came out as lesbian three years before, but
this was something else. Laurie was a child of the sixties.
She had gone through the whole rebellious scene, sampling
drugs, campus unrest, several years at a Hindu ashram, several affairs with young men, and a lengthy affair with an
older, married man. We were prepared for almost anything
as far as Laurie was concerned, because she had led us to
expect the unexpected.

*I am a retired New York City school teacher and an activist always fighting for human rights. For the past eleven years, I have been involved in the Soviet Jewry Movement. I was arrested for peacefully demonstrating in front of the Soviet Mission in Manhattan. As a volunteer, I have taught evening classes in English as a second language to immi-grants from all over the world. I love peo-ple, laughter, music and dance. My hus-band is an observant Jew and I keep kosher and observe the Sab-bath because it gives him joy. I am not a religious woman. I am a warm, caring and kind human being.*

The shock of Joyce's disclosure was much harder to handle than anything we had ever known. My first reaction was pain and hurt. How could she have kept this from us for so long? How could she not have trusted me? How she must have suffered when my husband and I spoke about our feelings regarding Laurie's lesbianism. Then I began to realize. Joyce couldn't have told us about herself after Laurie had come out to us. When she saw how devastated we were about Laurie, she had to be silent. How awful it must have been for her when she was forced to date the sons of my friends.

All of us, including Laurie, found it hard to believe that Joyce—the conservative religious, quiet girl—could be telling us that for many years she had known her preference for women, and that she only went out with men to please her father and me.

My husband, who is conservative and an Orthodox Jew, handled this situation beautifully and with a great deal of self-control. "Don't cry," he said. "We love you." And then, as if it were rehearsed, both of us said, "You're the same girl we've known and loved all of your life."

We talked, all five of us, around the table. We cried and we hugged and we kissed. A great deal of love was expressed and I could almost feel the relief that Joyce was experiencing. Whatever her father and I were feeling inwardly we kept well hidden and what she saw was a mother and father who loved her and accepted her sexual orientation. She didn't see the hurt and confusion that both of us were experiencing. We kept that inside ourselves until we went upstairs later that night.

That was a sleepless night during which we tried to find answers and tried to comfort one another. One thing we both agreed on was that we would give Joyce our support. My husband tried to tell me that it would all pass away like chicken pox or a bad cold, but I knew differently!

I thought back to the time when I learned about Laurie's

lesbianism. Laurie didn't "come out" exactly; it was when I visited her in Florida, where she was living with a female roommate, that I felt something strange and asked her about her relationship with this young woman. I could barely pronounce the word *lesbian;* it was such a dirty word to my way of thinking.

I was devastated to find out my suspicions were well-founded. I think this revelation hurt me more than her involvement in the drug scene and her last affair with the married man. It was all so alien to me. When I was fifteen, I read Radclyffe Hall's novel, *The Well of Loneliness,* but I didn't quite understand it. Other than that, all I knew was that lesbians were disgusting people, ugly women who wore men's clothes and did things to each other that were too horrible to talk about.

But this was something different. Laurie didn't fit my image of a lesbian as a woman who looked, acted, and dressed like a man. Laurie didn't fit this image at all. She was petite, pretty, bright and charming. Laurie had always attracted boys when she was young, and men when she grew older. What happened? Was it something I had done or hadn't done? How could I keep this horrible revelation from my Orthodox, conservative husband who looked forward to the day when Laurie would finally settle down with a nice Jewish boy and raise a family? Who could I speak to? What could I do? Nobody could be told. I had to keep this a secret and deal with it myself.

A busy person doesn't have too much time to brood over things. I was lucky. A full-time job, organization work and a family occupied most of my time. But the secret weighed heavily on my heart. The worst part was not having anyone to talk to. I had so many unanswered questions and so many fears. I looked for books dealing with the subject in the public library, but found nothing that helped in even a small way.

Eventually Laurie told her sister, Joyce, and so I was able to talk to her about some of my feelings. In retrospect, I can well imagine how Joyce must have suffered listening to me talk about Laurie.

Then my son was taken into our confidence and finally we all figured a way to break the news to Dad. My husband was angry. "It's a sickness," he said. "It's a result of all her crazy living." He absolutely refused to accept the fact that Laurie called herself a lesbian.

Two miserable years passed and then something wonderful happened. Laurie wrote asking me to come out to San Francisco and attend a conference of Jewish women, and I was able to go. From the first evening, when we attended a gay Shabbat, to the last evening four days later, I was on a merry-go-round. I attended as many workshops as was possible and even unexpectedly conducted one myself. Throughout the conference there was a great deal of warmth expressed. Many of my questions were answered and most of my fears were dispelled. I met lesbians from all walks of life, some with children, some who had been married for years before becoming lesbian, and some who were about to become mothers.

I came home as high as a kite. I was ready to shout out to all my friends and neighbors that my Laurie was fine! That I was no longer upset about the fact that she would never lead a "normal" life. That I was proud of all the things she was doing. That I liked her friends and that I loved her more than ever. I managed to convince my husband not to worry too much about Laurie, and both her sister and brother listened to my experiences with the gay women at the conference. They were pleased to find me in such a good frame of mind.

Then little by little, my joy dissipated. When I told my two closest friends about Laurie, both said they would not accept that kind of behavior and that I should forbid her to come into my home. I responded by putting these "friends" out of my life for almost a year. Only after they apologized profusely did I speak to them again. But our relationships will never be the same. When a third friend gave me similar advice, I decided not to speak truthfully to anyone about Laurie again. I think that I was so hurt and disappointed because I expected them to feel the way I was feeling after the conference. This is one of the hardest things I have had to cope with, responding to acquaintances and neighbors who constantly ask me if my daughters are married yet, or if I have any grandchildren.

There is also the religious aspect. While I seldom go to synagogue, my husband attends services every week. The rabbi, a young intelligent man, usually gives a series of lectures each year and I enjoy attending them with my husband. Imagine our feelings when, at the first session this year, he spoke about the blight on the New York Jewish community—lesbians and gay men! He said we must not allow them to teach in our schools and that we must keep them out of our synagogues. Both of us sat there sick at heart and couldn't wait to get home where we tried to deal with our feelings.

We love our daughters very much. This helps us deal with the many frustrations and heartaches we feel because their lives deviate from the norm. We worry about their futures. We are fortunate now that both Laurie and Joyce have lovers who are wonderful women. I am well aware of the fact that marriages don't last forever, but I do want our girls to have some stability in their lives. We're proud of them both as human beings. They are involved in worthwhile causes. They are loving, kind and considerate women and we are fortunate to have them. I hope that we will continue to be supportive of each other and that other parents of lesbians and gay men will help us create an environment of understanding so that all of our children can live with dignity and respect. I would like the world to accept my daughters, and others like them, for what they are and see them as I do: intelligent, warm, caring, wonderful women.

# From a Trunk to a Soapbox: An Update

*Since publication of the first edition of* Different Daughters, *Fran Harris has decided to come out—as Fran Salen.*

So much has happened to me since I wrote for *Different Daughters* ten years ago. I had been hiding in a locked trunk because I kept the knowledge of my daughter's lesbianism from my husband, family and friends. After I told my closest friend and she advised me to put my daughter out of my life, our friendship ended and I didn't dare tell anyone else.

The journey from a trunk to a soapbox was a difficult one, but the experiences I had along the way helped to make me a more knowledgeable, stronger and happier person.

Ten years ago, after I finally told my husband, he didn't accept my daughter's lesbianism at all. But through the years, both he and I listened, read and learned a great deal about homosexuality. My conservative Jewish husband even took part in a Gay and Lesbian Pride Day march, walking through the streets of San Francisco with other parents of homosexuals. But until his recent death, he still cherished the hope that one day both girls would tell us that it was just a phase and they were ready to meet and marry a good man and settle down in "normal lives."

I myself have changed completely, especially about keeping quiet. I speak out to others every chance I get. Even when the subject of homosexuality doesn't come up, I find myself speaking with authority. When it does come up, I contradict people who talk about the subject negatively and incorrectly. When someone expresses views that disturb me, I no longer cringe. I speak up and am invariably thanked for my candor. Often I am then told about a family member of theirs who is gay.

I now introduce my daughters' partners as my adopted daughters. I am close to the women they share their lives with and consider them part of my family. Fifteen year ago, I was pained to think I would not have grandchildren. Then a miracle happened. My youngest daughter's partner chose to become pregnant and was delivered a beautiful little girl who she named Ruth. She is a gift and a treasure. Ruth gives me great hugs and now says, "I love you, Grandma." Both my late husband and I were grateful to her mom for presenting us with this precious child.

Recently I spoke to a large group of women on the occasion of Mother's Day. I passed around photos of my daughters. Then I asked the women to tell me what they saw. They saw fine-looking, bright-eyed women. But they did not see lesbians. I began to talk, unrehearsed. I told them about my daughters' lives and partners. The group responded excitedly. They asked many questions, which I answered to the best of my ability.

I was thanked and asked for my number because many women felt there were other groups of women who would be interested in what I had to say about gay family members. Many women, including the woman who had asked me to speak, thanked me for clearing up misconceptions they had about gays and lesbians.

I have come a very long way. When neighbors or friends used to ask me about my daughters and whether they were married, I would avoid answering. "No, not yet," I'd say. Now I respond proudly. "Elizabeth is an attorney and her significant other is a chiropractor. They live together with my granddaughter, Ruth. Laurie is a social worker living in San Francisco with her partner, Kathry, a teacher at Stanford University. Both my daughters are lesbians."

I am comfortable and proud when I say this.

Lesbians and gay men do not have easy lives and I will do everything I can to see to it that they are afforded the right to live as equals in our society.

At the request of my husband, in the first book I did not reveal my real name. I used my maiden name so no one would recognize me. Now I want people to know who I am.

## Mary Dugan

## A Place at the Table

*I am a wife, mother, and high school English teacher living in Virginia. It means so much to me that my daughter wanted me to write an essay for this book. A few years ago, she would never have asked me to share my feelings.*

"Because I'm gay!" When these words exploded into the air in the middle of an argument, our world changed forever. In that instant, the one thing I knew was that, no matter what the situation, I loved my daughter unconditionally. That night, my feelings for this precious child were so strong I knew instinctively that even though we were all upset, somehow we would survive as a family. I did not know how we would survive, but I knew that we would.

Caroline came out to us in the heat of an argument when she was a senior in high school. However, her father, David, and I had been concerned about her emotional health since her freshman year. When Caroline began high school, we felt that her world changed. She had always been a bright, fun-loving girl, but as she reached her teens, we saw her become depressed. At first, we blamed the changes on her heavy honors course load and the challenges of attending a large high school. Next, we blamed her new friends. Caroline had always had a wonderful group of friends around her, but when she went to the new school, she met new friends. Two of these friends, whom we loved, had some emotional problems. In fact, one of them became so depressed that she considered suicide and was eventually hospitalized. Caroline had been privy to this friend's suicide wishes, and the responsibility of this information was too much for Caroline. She, too, became depressed.

I now feel that we did not treat Caroline's mental health seriously enough. After taking her to a psychiatrist who said she was not suicidal, we were relieved and went on about our business. I believe good therapy at this time would have helped Caroline deal with her own concerns about her sexuality which, we now know, were beginning to surface. Even though I have always felt that we are a close family, she probably felt that sharing feelings about her gender identification was impossible. Thus, in the middle of our busy lives, even though Caroline was probably feeling confused, we said that everything was alright, and we proceeded with our activities. At this time, my husband changed jobs, and although moves are not easy for teenagers even in the best of circumstances, we moved to Virginia.

In Virginia, the girls found a lot of good friends and a receptive community. Yet, to David and me, Caroline still seemed troubled and immature for her age. Outwardly, she had many friends and found much academic and social success in her new situation. In fact, when she "came out" to her friends two years after our move, she found support from her friends, her teachers, and other adults that she knew. The support of these people sustained her before she told her father and me. I know that some people did hurt her with words, but basically she was still "Caroline" to all who cared for her. For that acceptance, we will always be grateful.

Telling the narrative leading up to Caroline's coming out to us is the easy part. Discussing what has happened in my life since that day is more difficult. I wish that I could say that I only reacted with positive words of encouragement and understanding, but I can't. I did react with love, but I also reacted, I think quite naturally, with anger, disbelief, and grief. After all, our hopes and dreams of what life would be like for our daughter changed dramatically. We had to replace pictures of her idyllic life with a professional job, husband, and family with pictures of possible discrimination, alienation, and rejection by some parts of society.

What would happen to this precocious young woman who wanted so desperately to make a contribution to the world? Could she fulfill those goals? Would the world allow her to, or would she be thwarted and put down until she became a negative influence instead of a positive one? All of these questions and a hundred more troubled my husband and me. What about Emily, her sister, two years younger than Caroline? How would this news impact her? How could our family possibly come together?

After her senior year, Caroline went to a small liberal arts college where she thought she would find a welcoming community and where she felt her writing could blossom. However, after a year and a half, she decided that she would like to attend a women's college, so she transferred to Smith College in Northampton, Massachusetts. Sending her to a private school has been a financial strain on our family, but we feel good that in this school she has found an accepting community and a place that nurtures her academic interests. She loves college, and I believe that she will embark on a career that will help others and that will foster acceptance and understanding among all people.

For our family, this progression to her senior year has not been easy. We have survived. If I were to live these last four years over, I would seek more family counseling for all of us. Even though we would probably end up where we are today, I think the journey would have been less painful. Interspersed with the good times were times when there was very little communication between us. There was a period during which Caroline left school for a year to explore "the real world" in San Francisco. I assume much of the responsibility for our communication breakdown; I was a controlling mother and wanted Caroline to make the decisions I would make. Nevertheless, each turn that we thought was a negative has been one that provided growth for Caroline and for the rest of us. For example, letting her spend her summers working in Provincetown, Massachusetts allowed her to be enveloped by an accepting community. Because she was only nineteen when she first went to the Cape, we worried about negative influences that she might encounter in this liberal atmosphere. While visiting her there that first summer, I knew we had made the right decision in letting her go when some of her friends said that they wished they could be more open with their parents and bring them to Provincetown. Watching Caroline struggle to mature has been hard for us, I have not always agreed with every decision she has made, but I have watched her interact with her friends and I am glad that she allows us to meet her friends and take part in her life.

Talking with Caroline is not always easy. We still disagree; but unlike two years ago, Caroline allows us to disagree and discuss issues. I used to feel that she felt that her lesbianism was the bottom line in every issue that we discussed. I used to feel that I had to measure every word that I said to her because I was afraid that I would upset her or give her the wrong impression of my feelings. I also felt that I had to mask my feelings, but I now feel fairly comfortable talking with her about most anything. I am so glad that we have reached this place of understanding; the suicide rate among young gay and lesbian people who feel that they can't share their thoughts and feelings alarms me.

Growing up, Caroline was always active in our church activities. As a teenager, she became a committed Christian and attended our church as well as that of her best friends. When we moved to Virginia, she continued to be a leader in church activities, and she encouraged ecumenical functions among teens in our town. Once she accepted that she was gay, however, she seemed to turn from the organized church. At first, I was not too concerned because young people often question their faith during the teen years.

But now, it seems Caroline has rejected organized religion. I think she sees the church as hypocritical and unaccepting of all people, and in many instances, she is correct. I also believe that she feels that God has rejected her because she is gay. I understand why she feels this rejection, but I wish she would realize that even though some *people* may have rejected her, God has not. With some more time to mature and reflect, she may realize this.

I am glad that Caroline can talk with me and even ask my advice on occasion! Every conversation is no longer a battle or a test; she knows that I love her and that I will support her; she doesn't have to test limits any longer. I may not always agree with her; my beliefs on some issues might be very different from hers. Nevertheless, our love allows us to respect each other's right to her own views.

Even though most everyone close to our family knows that Caroline has "come out," we have not been able to tell my parents. David's family has been very supportive and understanding, but I am afraid that my parents would suffer because they simply couldn't understand the whole concept of homosexuality. In an effort to spare them worry, we have chosen not to tell them at this time, but not telling them has built an invisible wall between us. Many days, I feel that Caroline should come out to them. She need not fear that they will reject her. She knows that, yet she wants to spare them worry and concern for her well-being.

Today, I look forward to the time when the four of us can be closer. We are at peace and we are a family; because the girls have been away at college, we have not had a lot of "quality time." I anticipate that these next years will be ones in which we look at each other through more understanding, more empathetic eyes. This life we are given to lead is hard, but the more problems I encounter, the more opportunities I have to realize that people really are more alike than they are different. I am thankful for all of the people in my life who have let me talk, cry and laugh with them. They have helped me see Caroline, Emily, and David for who they really are—my kind, loving family.

I am not sure that I have said anything that will help other mothers of "different daughters," but I can say that just writing down my thoughts and feelings has been cathartic; I recommend writing to anyone who is trying to cope with change within her family. If I had written this two years ago, it would have been full of more specific examples of my failures and successes in dealing with Caroline. Today, what is important to me is that Caroline is her own person; she loves us, she trusts us, and she is willing to have us in her life. I am so proud of all that she has accomplished at college and look forward to watching her develop as a constructive member of our society. I know she has a lot to give to all of us. I may never fully understand her, but I will love her. I am glad that she has her family and friends to call upon. Hearing stories of her friends who cannot talk to their parents makes me realize how lucky we are.

Ellen Goodman, a columnist, wrote recently about families in her editorial, "Diversity Is All in the Family":

> In families, our children first struggle with the need to be themselves and to belong. At the kitchen table, we first find out if we can be accepted as who we are and still be connected to others.
>
> When families work, they acknowledge individuality, make room for difference, weave family stories out of eccentricities. When families work, the members make a commitment to stay at the table.

I hope that our family will always be centered around God, love, and a commitment to each other.

# Choices and Surprises

LETICIA WILEY

*I am from the Philippines and came to the United States as a student. At twenty-two, I married a white American, Sasha's father. We divorced eleven years later. I have a PhD in Sociology but never really used it, as the job market for sociologists collapsed after I graduated. I had a career in banking, but quit four years ago and started to write fiction.*

I found out that Sasha is a lesbian a little over a year ago. She is the second of three children and she was then twenty-eight. How did I find out? We were at home doing the Tarot and I did a spread for Sasha. A significant card came up, the card of judgement. In this card, there are gray-colored people rising from their tombs, while above is an angel with a trumpet. I told Sasha the card meant people were being called to change, to be reborn. The people on the card were leaving their tombs to become liberated.

Sasha brightened up. Another card showed. The queen of Pentacles. Sasha saw the card and said, "I'm in love." She pointed to the card with the queen and said "I'm in love with her." She looked at me, and I got it!

I was stunned. At the same time I felt relief, for her and the rest of the family. Sasha had been leading a secret life for three or four years. We never saw her and though we lived close to each other, we could never find her. It was even hard to reach her by telephone. She was very elusive. I worried about her all the time. I imagined that she was on drugs, or in bad company, or in trouble of some sort. A woman kept turning up, a sort of special friend, but I didn't read anything into it. Looking back, I think this may have been her first lesbian relationship. I don't know how long it lasted or when it started.

On the day we did the Tarot and Sasha finally allowed me into her private life, I felt happy and relieved. She no longer felt the need for secrets! I was also happy because she had found someone to love and love her back. I told my husband (Sasha's stepfather since she was nine, someone who's been a parent to her as much as I have) that we should bring the family together to mark the news and celebrate Sasha's coming out. We rented a beach house for a long weekend and called the rest of the family, Sasha's brother and sister. We also told our friends. I said Sasha was a lesbian, that she had a sweetheart, and that we were going to meet her!

At that time, Sasha and Jess had known each other for several months. They met "just like in the movies." Sasha was driving an airport shuttle and Jess was a passenger. My first impression of Jess was of radiant, glowing health—she's tall, red-headed, and very athletic. She's also very sweet, and my heart went out to her at once. I thought she and Sasha looked great together.

Sasha is a wonderful daughter and I am so happy she has found her path. She is no different now than she was before, but I do worry about her having difficulties along this path. I am going to do my best to help her. It's almost as if she said to me, "Mom, I'm going to be a lawyer and I'm going to need help through law school." Of course, I don't know how I would have reacted if she had told us she was a lesbian when she was a teenager. I took into account that she was in her late twenties and had been trying to find herself for a long time. Though we are now close, I miss the years we lost, the years when she was keeping secrets and figuring out her life. It took so long for her to come out to herself, let alone to tell us. I can't help thinking how much courage it took. And I also feel pain, thinking what a long and lonely struggle it must have been.

My strongest feeling now is great joy and relief that Sasha has found herself. She is in a much better place now that she knows who she is. I never felt like I had to judge her. She is our daughter, a gentle, kind, funny and generous woman. She's a lesbian. So what?

I called my sister in the Philippines to tell her about Sasha. She didn't say much, but urged me not to tell our father. Her attitude seemed to indicate that something like this could happen in America, but not in the Philippines, and that my father, now in his late eighties, would not understand. Maybe my sister is right. With anybody else I have no problem saying my daughter is a lesbian and that she has a sweetheart. I expect some difficulties when I go to the Philippines and my father asks me about Sasha. As of now, after more than a year since Sasha came out to us, I still don't know how, or if, I should tell my father.

In the Philippines, people joke about homosexuality. They will point rudely at an effeminate man or say they are sorry for his parents. The culture is not friendly to homosexuality. Although Filipinos do not engage in physical gay bashing, they feel free to snigger, joke, and make fun of homosexuals. Now I find this behavior very offensive.

I think everybody here who knows Sasha knows about her life. I've told all our friends that Sasha has come out as a gay woman, that she has a wonderful sweetheart. If I don't mind, why should they? One woman asked why I was so cheerful. I said that Sasha had been struggling to find out who she was, now that she knows the answer, I'm very happy for her. Maybe some people find my attitude objectionable, but if so, I doubt they would say anything to my face. They just have to learn. Jess comes to all our family events. I wouldn't dream of excluding her. She is as much a part of our family as my son's fiancée. Sasha loves Jess, so we love Jess, too. It's very simple.

I came from a culture where parents still make choices about their children's lives. In America, children are more free to express their personalities and make their own choices. This sometimes leads to surprises, but I think life is better that way.

HAZEL BRICKMAN

# From Hermit Crabs to Hamsters

*I am seventy-four, married, and live with my husband. I have two children, a daughter, forty-three, and a son, thirty-six, and three teenage grandchildren. I was a high school speech teacher for about forty years, and for the most part loved it. In my retirement, I have been involved in Elderhostel Programs (continuing education), yoga, tutoring at the Fortune Society for ex-convicts, traveling, playing tennis, and swimming and sunning in California. Also, I love to eat!*

Dear Louise,

This account of my recollections of the history of the relationship with my lesbian daughter will be in the form of a letter to you. I feel I'll be speaking to a most accepting listener.

First, the facts of the situation. After eleven years of marriage and three children, my daughter fell in love with a mother of three children, married fourteen years. Within one month of physically consummating their relationship, my daughter told me about it. Partly, she told me because she and her husband were requesting financial assistance, thinking their marriage might be saved through counseling. Secondly—and this I'm proud of—she knew I would continue to love and accept her, although her lover feared anger and rejection. The remaining facts—both women divorced their husbands and set up a joint household, with two mothers, six children from age three to eleven, and varied pets, from hermit crabs to hamsters. Both at that time retained custody of their children, although the husbands were aware of the lesbian relationship and held it over them in one way or another.

That was about twelve years ago. I can remember, vividly, her taking me for a walk on a misty, summer afternoon when I was visiting her in the country. She indicated she felt an explanation was due me and her dad as to why her marriage seemed to be floundering. She then explained that she had been unhappy for the entire eleven years of her marriage, had never felt she could tell me, and in the past two years had found a warm, responsive relationship—with another woman—and named her, someone I had known as a close friend of hers. And then she added, most helpfully, "You know, Mom, I'm exactly the same loving daughter that I was five minutes ago, before you knew of this relationship."

First there was shock, for although she had been the tomboy, athletic-type all her life, she had also been very popular with boys and men and had appeared deeply in love with the husband she married. My second reaction was relief. At last the husband whom we felt had never been a compatible choice, would now, probably, be out of the picture. As for the relationship with the woman, we didn't think it likely to continue. It just seemed too out of character for a daughter of ours to be romantically involved with a woman. How little we knew; how little we understood!

The request from my daughter was to convey this information to her dad. With my head spinning from this turn of events, I returned home that evening and promptly, as gently as I could, using very much my daughter's approach, told my husband. He was flabbergasted and puzzled; tended to believe his daughter had been seduced; was hopeful that she would terminate her marriage; and quite sure, as I was, that this was a "passing fancy" caused by an unhappy marriage.

During the next few years, while I read furiously everything I could find (and my daughter fed me plenty of printed material), her father became bitterly rejecting of her lover. He couldn't abide her personality, even before he knew of the relationship with our daughter. He was sure she was a seductress—and he vetoed her inclusion in family gatherings at our home. This caused deep anguish to my daughter, myself and her lover, and, I'm sure, to my husband.

Our daughter's brother, seven years younger than she, and in his early twenties when she divorced, was baffled by the events. How had she chosen the wrong husband and had three children by him? So my husband and I told him the truth. He had no problems accepting his sister, and now understood the divorce. She eventually talked fully and frankly with him so that, for the first time, brother and sister felt very close.

One of the most difficult episodes was the upset experienced by my husband and I when she told us she had agreed to "come out" on a television program dealing with the civil rights of lesbian mothers. We feared for her job in the New York City school system; we feared rejection of her by students and fellow workers; we feared the effect on her children in their relationships with their peers.

We watched the half-hour program—on a major network—with trepidation. However, we wound up feeling pride in her contribution to the cause of civil liberties, a cause which we had always championed. Not only did she not lose face in the teaching community, but her administration, wisely, recognized her insights so that she was asked to be a resource person for gay and lesbian students with problems.

There was to be a repeat of the program the following week. This time we called friends and relatives, none of whom, to our knowledge, had been aware of her lesbianism, and urged them to watch. To our amazement, we discovered for ourselves the tremendous relief of being "out of the closet." There were only positive results. We were surrounded by wonderful friends who expressed their support.

One area of difficulty, however, was between my husband and myself. I was able to accept our daughter's choice of a mate, although I disapproved strongly of many of this woman's attitudes and ethics, whereas, for my husband, she was an anathema. He had to reject her as a physical presence, not because of her homosexuality, but because of her personality. Because I knew how deeply our daughter felt this rejection of her choice, I suffered her pain, my husband's and my own. It was an unhappy time. The only resolution for this was to spend time with my daughter and her lover alone, without involving my husband.

There were also concerns about how the children—growing into their teens—would handle their mother's lifestyle. We need not have worried. Now, at fourteen, seventeen and nineteen, they appear to be typical, average teenagers, with their typical problems and pursuits.

On the whole, I have found that because my daughter is "out," I am freed so that I may speak up when I hear a homophobic comment. I can educate where I hear lack of information, and I can support where I sense a need.

My life has been enriched by knowing gay and lesbian individuals. Never have I been so close to my daughter, or so able to be honest with her. I can truly say I'm grateful she has found a healthy expression for her sexuality, now with a warm, loving person. I have to say it has made the whole family relationship a happier one, because we find the present person in my daughter's life so wonderful and she is part of our family circle. Our daughter is living a rich, rewarding life with the same level of energy and capability she has always displayed, but with the solid assurance that she has her parents' admiring support.

I appreciate this opportunity to share these experiences in a steadily-strengthening relationship with my daughter.

DORIS THOMPSON

# A Tradition of Strength

*I am a black woman, fifty-three years old, a graduate of a women's college. I am retired from almost thirty years of federal service, the last ten years of which were spent in equal employment and civil rights work. I'm now working independently as an organization consultant, conducting training and management consultations around people problems. I have worked and lived in mixed racial and gender situations all my life. I feel I have an open philosophy about looking at various lifestyles, how people live and what people want.*

Despite my open mind, my first reaction to Margaret's lesbianism was to think it was another life phase for her. The child of a broken marriage, she had recently moved back from living with her father. Our relationship was improving, but it wasn't all that good. I didn't even know she was thinking about coming out. Thinking her lesbianism a stage was the extent of my openness, and I stayed at that point for quite a while. I think now, two years later, I am really just moving out of that attitude. More than just a lifestyle, I now know lesbianism is the way she wants to live, the way she sees herself, the way she is.

I have always had strong role models in my life, grandmothers and great aunts who I saw working and who were not in traditional women's roles—even in their marriages. One of my grandmothers raised her five children as a single parent. She was widowed and though she remarried—unheard of at the time—she later divorced. She was really the matriarch of the family. I think this all has something to do with Margaret and her lifestyle. I love women, and I respect women who are assertive and powerful.

I didn't feel threatened by her choice, but I really wondered how she knew, how she made the decision. We've talked about women being strong and powerful, but that doesn't mean all strong women are lesbians. Many of the qualities about lesbians that she has discussed with me are ones I have seen in a lot of women, and I haven't necessarily thought these women were lesbians. I have these qualities, yet I am a straight woman. That's the part that is still confusing to me.

I didn't ask Margaret directly why she was a lesbian. Now that I have learned more of the things she feels, I think there are a lot of things in her life experience that could have led her to that decision. In me, she has a strong role model and she has a grandmother who has been politically active all her life. Margaret's own politics and deep convictions about social responsibility certainly must have contributed to her choice.

Margaret keeps asking me who I have told about her. I have problems about this. If I tell people, they want explanations. It puts you in such a position. I talked about it as if it were a stage with the first friend I told. I still have problems saying, "My daughter is a lesbian."

Margaret loves children and plans to have some, which I feel really good about. When the time comes that she is going to have a child, adopt a child, or raise a child, I know it will bring up the issue with lots of people. Margaret has not yet told her grandmothers and I wouldn't see that as my role, but I do think I could talk to my mother about it, and I know that time will come. I know that I am not ashamed of her. I am very proud of her and who she is. Margaret is my daughter and I love her. That love hasn't changed, and never will.

I have met many of Margaret's friends, other women whom I want to know and be around. Visiting with her has been so good, though we all do have such stereotypes! It's almost like the way people think about blacks. I guess I see a lot of similarities in the way we look at lots of people. If you don't experience things with people, you think of them as strange or different and therefore you are afraid of them. We have to learn about the lesbian lifestyle. I have much to learn, but I think basically we are all people. We all feel love and pain. We all experience relationships, and there are only degrees of difference between us. My learning about her life is an evolutionary process.

LOIS YOUNG-TULIN

# Movement and Change

*I live in the Philadelphia area. A writer and teacher, I have published numerous poems and articles, as well as the book* Escape Roots *(1994). I have been named University Scholar in the Teaching of Writing at Antioch University.*

The women's movement swept me up at a time when I was living in suburban Philadelphia with three children. I had married young; by 1972, I had a ten-year-old daughter, Karen, and two sons, seven and four. I enrolled in an adult degree program, mainly because it required only two annual on-campus residencies, with the rest of the academic work done independently. Before my first residency, I was faced with the tremendous task of cooking and freezing fourteen dinners, shopping for a full two weeks' worth of food and household supplies, and arranging for live-in child care to help my husband while I was off studying. By the time I arrived at college, I was totally exhausted from these preparations and the accompanying guilt that I felt leaving my three children and my husband for what was only fourteen days.

During those two weeks, I lived and studied with women from all over the globe who were deep into the women's movement and who quickly turned my head around. The experience changed the course of my life. I realized many things during that two-week respite from suburban life. I found out that I was valuable and talented, yet oppressed. I came to realize I deserved equality in the home, in the workplace, and in my everyday life. What followed after my return to Philadelphia was my quick agreement to join a women's group, and a determination to change my oppressive life with more equity in child care, housekeeping, and career goals.

By 1975, I had a BA degree, an MA degree, a full-time

faculty position, and an active political life in the women's and local anti-war movements. And then, in 1976, my husband and I legally and amicably separated. Karen was just completing her junior year of high school; I was proud of Karen—proud of her developing feminism, pleased with her acceptance at an excellent college.

At college, Karen met Peter, and within a year's time, they were sharing a dormitory room. I liked Peter. He seemed like a non-oppressive male partner, the kind of man my daughter deserved. Meanwhile, Karen wrote that she was very active at the Womyn's Center at college. I sensed that she was a rooted feminist, sure of herself, strong in her beliefs and capable. What more could I, a born-again feminist, want for my daughter?

Several years later, Karen and Peter were obviously growing apart, and Karen was going through a sexual revolution of her own—not sure if she were gay or straight. It was May of 1983 when Karen came out to me. Intellectually, I accepted this, but emotionally, my reaction even shocked myself! Hadn't she loved Peter, a male? Hadn't she always loved boys, worried about dates and being popular? I was disappointed in myself for being upset. After all, I was a fierce supporter of lesbian rights, and my own women's group (still going strong after over ten years) was made up of lesbians as well as straight women.

I was devastated, nevertheless. *My* daughter? I went through a shame/blame syndrome and wondered what I had done wrong. Did my own radical feminism cause Karen to rebel by being more outrageous and declaring herself a lesbian? I was convinced she was merely going through a phase, that she would play it out and then return to heterosexuality. I talked to no one about her coming out to me, afraid that telling someone would make it fact and would mark her for life. If she changed back to men it would be too late once word got around. How homophobic I was! Looking back, I am both shocked and ashamed of these reactions. But they were my real feelings and thoughts, and, if nothing else, I was being honest with myself.

After her graduation from college in June of 1984, Karen moved back in with me. Although I confessed to her that I was reading a few books for parents of gay children, I still hoped her lesbianism would go away. I knew better intellectually, academically, objectively—but emotionally I was coping poorly, buying into the homophobia all around me. I thought Karen was acting out and rebelling because of my feminism and divorce. Emotionally I was stuck. No one else in the family or in our immediate circle knew about her lesbianism. Not her father, not her brothers, not my mother, no one—except Karen's friends. Was I protecting Karen or protecting myself?

A friend had a gay son, but I didn't even tell this friend that Karen had come out to me. I was in a state of denial, convincing myself that if I didn't mention it, it would go away. I was deeply in the closet as a mother of a gay child. I felt ashamed, fearful, guilty, all wrapped into one package—and silence and mourning was my mask for anger and self-blame.

"I haven't come out to Dad yet," she told me one day.

"Were you planning to?"

"Do you think I should?" she asked me.

"It's not an easy subject for him."

In November of 1984, Karen came home from having dinner with her father and staying overnight at his apartment. "Well," she said, "I came out to Dad, and he seemed okay with it."

She and I hugged, and I felt as though I finally didn't have to carry this burden alone. Now he and I could talk about how it felt to be parents of a lesbian. I hadn't told him myself for several reasons, mainly because I felt it was Karen's choice and responsibility to tell him, not mine. Now Karen was telling me that she had come out to her father, and he had been fine with it. Good news.

Then I received a telephone call from him. He wanted to

meet with Karen and me to discuss this "horrible situation." He felt as if Karen and I had conspired against him, kept her lesbianism a secret on purpose, and said he and I had better start collaborating and putting an end to this nonsense immediately! He invited me to accompany him on a visit to his therapist.

The following day we went to see Dr. B. who told us that, if we moved fast, we could do something about Karen's acting like a lesbian. The fact that she wasn't and as of yet had not been in a primary relationship with a woman meant that she wasn't sold on her own lesbianism, he said, and we had to nip this thing in the bud. We set a date for a three-way meeting with Karen. Dr. B. had stressed one thing: It was important that we united on this issue, and were not at odds with each other. Under no circumstances should we argue with each other in Karen's presence.

The three of us met on the first floor of my center city house. We sat in the parlor, Karen in a chair and my ex-husband and I on either end of a couch. My ex did most, if not all, of the talking. He screamed at Karen for acting out in this vile, destructive manner and said he thought she had aimed it at ruining his name and reputation in Philadelphia. He vowed to disown her and cut her off from the family. I sat in total silence, stunned by his reaction. I tensed up, got a violent headache, and blocked out his words. He ranted and raved about how I had conspired with our daughter against him, determined to shame him and keep the facts from him. And I whimped out on my daughter, so totally disarmed, unprepared and shocked was I from this unexpected turn of events. I suspected that Karen took my silence to mean that I agreed with her father, that I, too, would disown her. But I thought once we got him out of there, I'd hug her and burst into tears. During that meeting, all I wanted to do was to cry, but even my tears were dried up and silenced. What was wrong with me? I felt paralyzed, as if I had been injected with a drug that left me immobile. As it had when I was a young wife and mother, his ranting and raving left me numb, speechless and spaced out. I was totally confused, and felt crazy!

It was a terrible episode that would greatly damage my relationship with my daughter. Where was my voice? Where was my feminism and mothering instincts? I wanted to shrivel up in an invisible ball and die! Dr. B. had stressed the importance of our standing united. I had thought he was the informed professional and I should do as he said.

Meanwhile, Karen sought the help of a therapist to cope with the pain of her parents' reaction. She asked me to accompany her to one of her sessions. During that therapy session, Karen cried and accused me of abandoning her. She was right in accusing me, and I told her so. The therapist helped me explore what had rendered me numb and mute during that meeting and helped me apologize to Karen. It didn't completely heal the pain, but did alleviate some of Karen's feeling of being ganged up on by her parents.

I felt it was important, however, for Karen to keep up a relationship with her father, and I encouraged Karen to call him around the New Year and wish him the best. She did, hoping I was giving her sound guidance, only to be rebuked by his curt thank you. Later that year, Karen, her father and I went out to lunch. I wanted to break the ice between them, get things rolling in terms of putting them back in contact, then step out of their way, hoping they could heal their relationship. The only way he would agree to see Karen was if I was there. I feared the old scenario again, but we all went. We made small talk, but at least the lines of communication were opened. Afterwards, he would occasionally call Karen, or visa versa, just to say hello and make more small talk, which was better than no talk at all.

That year was full of change. With each passing month, I was coming out of denial, passing through mourning, and approaching acceptance as the mother of a lesbian. Soon Karen began dating and bringing women home. That July she had a lesbian birthday party in my house, and I liked most of the guests. They were, on the whole, wonderful close friends to Karen, bright, caring, loving women of varied ages and cultural backgrounds, many graduate students, lawyers, social workers, teachers, salespeople, and some unemployed. I began to feel good about Karen's sexual orientation. Karen became more open with me about her relationships, and I became more accepting.

And Karen's father, who had needed some catch-up time to deal with being the parent of a gay child, is slowly accepting our daughter's partner and sexual orientation. He is finally proud of Karen's scholarship, career, ethical strength and humanity. Occasionally, things still come up, moments of awkwardness with friends, reactions to news events, and sadness for the dream he had once had for his daughter. They come up for me, the initial awkwardness when I interrupt another person's homophobic joke, the risk I sometimes feel when I come out to an older generation aunt, but the truthfulness sits well with my sense of integrity and pride, and love for my daughter.

It is now ten years since Karen came out. She lives in San Francisco with her female partner. Karen, her partner and I get along famously, and I call myself J's mother-in-law. I march in gay rights parades; I support gay and lesbian rights, and I am open about being the mother of a lesbian. Karen is a fabulous, loving, talented woman whom I love very much, and I am extremely proud of her.

RHODA RAFKIN

# After the Initial Shock

A few years ago, I received a letter from my daughter, Louise, who was living in New Zealand, hinting that she was in a relationship with a woman. At that particular time, my reaction was shock, since she had been in a relationship with a male New Zealander for about five years and I was very fond of him. After the initial shock, I felt that it was something she was going through but I also remember thinking, "I don't need another problem, why can't my kids be normal?"

I was born and brought up in a very straight-laced New England town where homosexuality wasn't even discussed in "polite society" and this new revelation was a bit shocking. In the early forties, we lived on a Navy base where the military fired a lot of lesbians because their alleged "loose morals" marked them as security risks. I had very negative impressions about lesbians, and all I could think of was that they were perverts, more or less. From reading psychology books, I also thought they were women who had bad relationships with their fathers, or men in general, and Louise had some very pleasant experiences with men and got on well with her father. I just didn't know what else to think. One of my dearest friends lives in New Zealand and she wrote and said what wonderful friends my

*After my husband died, I returned to teaching full-time. For many years, I taught emotionally disturbed youngsters and brain-damaged college students, but am now a marine biology instructor at a marine institute where we see many thousands of children of all ages, introducing them to the excitement of the ecology and animals of the oceans. I love to travel and go to school. Over the past ten years, I've studied a strange array of subjects, from ceramics to Chinese cooking, sailing to sign language. There is never enough time to do all the things I want to do!*

daughter had, and that I needn't worry about her. That was very important to me.

I knew Louise was very committed to the women's movement, and I thought maybe this relationship with a woman was one of her strong statements, since she never does things half-way. I certainly hoped it was merely a "statement," and she did state in her letters that some of her actions were political. I went to check out some information on the subject of lesbianism and couldn't find one good book in our local conservative small town library. All the while in the back of my mind, I kept thinking it would go away with time. Louise was so far away, and I didn't have to face the reality of the situation.

Being widowed for several years, I felt the need for someone to confide in. I am really fortunate in having two wonderfully kind and compassionate women friends with whom I talked. We came to the conclusion that Louise was: a) being influenced by other women who felt oppressed by men; b) rebelling (but we weren't sure against what or whom); or c) asserting her independence. But certainly she could not be a "true" lesbian; that we couldn't accept!

In December of that year, I visited Louise in New Zealand, met her friends and saw how she lived. I found her friends intelligent, talented, loyal, loving and caring women. I found that by being involved in her life, I could become more accepting and more able to understand her and her beliefs. I also began to face the fact that her way of life was not going to go away. One of the most memorable nights I had in New Zealand was a particular New Year's Eve that my friend and I spent tending bar at a lesbian dance. It's an experience neither of us will ever forget. It was my first initiation into lesbian social life and it was a rude awakening for me to see women dancing and being affectionate together. It wasn't a world I was familiar with, but it was one I could accept. This year I was in New Zealand again, camping with my friend, and we talked about the lesbian dance and all the fun times we have had with Louise and her friends.

Since then I have gone through a period of soul-searching and growth in accepting Louise's lifestyle as is. However, this might have been a different story had my husband been alive. I believe that he would have found his daughter's lesbianism difficult to handle and this would have been a struggle for me. I wouldn't want to be put in the middle of them, and though I don't think he would have loved her any less, I think it would have been hard for him at first.

My son, who is thirty-two, dearly loves his sister but finds it difficult to accept her lifestyle. He is involved in golf, surfing and fishing, and goes about with a group of macho young men. I think that as time passes and their understanding and communication improves, he will find it easier to accept.

I do have uncomfortable feelings when I see Louise displaying affection publicly with another woman, and I haven't delved into why it offends me since I am very fond of her friends. Once when she was visiting home, she kissed her lover in front of the house and I felt really uncomfortable. I am aware of the neighbors, and people talking. When I am in Oakland, where Louise lives, it doesn't bother me so much because gay lifestyles are more accepted there. I have decided to handle life with my neighbors and acquaintances by not making my daughter's sexual choice a matter of discussion. I am aware that people probably have figured it out on their own. Some of my neighbors have lived here for over twenty years and I am sure they see Louise as a great person without judging her on her sexual preference.

While I love her, accept her, and admire Louise's wonderful qualities and accomplishments, I still struggle with the outside world of acquaintances and relatives who are prejudiced against lesbian lifestyles. It is hard for me to deal with their disapproval—perhaps due to a lack of courage on my part. She recently "came out" at her high school reunion, and though this is a very small town, nothing has come back to me about her lesbianism.

This year I went to the Gay Day parade, and though I enjoyed myself, there were parts of it which offended me: some of the women on motorcycles, some of the men in women's clothing. The negative parts stand out in my mind because I felt it was a perfect place to show the world how gays and lesbians are not so different from others. I loved other parts of the parade, all the AIDS help groups and the social and political groups. I think lesbians and gays are more concerned with social and political issues—the world as a whole, not just the gay world—than are straight people. I can only judge this by my daughter's friends, but I feel this is true.

Louise and I have a very special relationship. We are good friends and she has taught me a lot. I think we sincerely admire each other. Our times together are filled with challenges, common interests and vitality. I think she desires for me to be as militant as she is about social issues. I understand her zeal, however, I have my own style of concern and action. Rather than by being militant, I find that by showing my self-reliance and taking challenges, I can be a strong example of an independent woman. Yet, I also find that by being so self-sufficient, I am very lonely at times. The men of my generation do not want an Amazon woman, rather they prefer someone to dominate and look after in return for nurturing.

When I look over the past few years, my life seems to have taken a journey of self-examination and adaptation of my attitudes. I constantly sort and sift through them in order to be at peace with myself. There are still things about lesbians I don't understand, the sexual part for one, and I still find myself wondering how Louise *knew* she was lesbian. But I have had a lot of opportunities to be around many types of lesbians of all ages. I have stayed at my daughter's house, visited other lesbians, gone camping with them. I think it's important for mothers to be with their daughters in their own surroundings and get to know their friends. I think as we mothers find out that our daughters are really in very good company, we can feel better. For me, understanding has come through knowledge plus faith, lots of struggles, and most importantly, love.

## After *Different Daughters:* An Update

Ten years after Louise's book came out, my friend Ruth and I are on a camping trip. Ruth, my dear friend, is from New Zealand, and since Louise came out there, she has been involved in Louise's lesbian lifestyle since the beginning. Louise dedicated the first book to both of us. Ruth has always enjoyed a warm relationship with Louise and is grateful for the chance to see another way of life.

"Louise and her many interesting friends have added a dimension to my life for which I am most thankful," she says setting down her orange juice on our camp table.

*Rhoda Rafkin is still teaching and has become a grandmother twice. She has travelled to Alaska and China and is fascinated by computers. She is now "on-line" communicating with Louise via e-mail.*

*Ruth Broughten lives in New Zealand and spends several months each year in the States, visiting her son, his wife and new grandchild, and Rhoda. Her other son lives in New Zealand with his partner.*

We are finishing a "gourmet" camp breakfast, looking out at the Pacific Ocean, and reminiscing about our families and friends. Our thoughts eventually turn to Louise's lifestyle and we find most of our thoughts are positive.

Would Louise have been any different if she had not come out? We don't really think so. Her path may have been different, but we both feel she would still have had the same successful career as a writer, journalist and self-defense instructor. She is involved in community activities and social causes, which she would have been whatever her sexual preference.

Over the years, we have met Louise's many friends, from all over this country and Europe. We have been struck by their warmth, caring and concern. Professionally and personally, they all stand out as wonderful people.

Louise questions us about why we don't ask about her relationships. In that foreign territory, we are unsure of ourselves and fear that we may be prying into areas that are too personal. We don't usually ask our heterosexual friends about personal relationships, either. We listen, and given an opportunity, are happy to talk and discuss her life, but in most instances we find it difficult to take an initiative lest we offend. It is not that we lack interest in Louise and her friends and lovers—they have always been welcome wherever we are. We consider them our friends as well.

This summer we enjoyed a few weeks together on Nantucket where we have family. Our extended family is very accepting of Louise and her current partner, and really enjoy their company. We also spent some time with Louise in her environment, Provincetown, Massachusetts, an insightful experience for two gray-haired New England women! On summer nights, the streets are filled with gay men and lesbians of all kinds.

We were treated to a weekly bocce ball tournament of Louise's friends. We cheered on both teams of lesbians. The camaraderie of these young women was apparent. Winners or losers, everyone earned a big hug.

That night we went to a local cabaret to hear a lesbian comic. Here, we had mixed feelings. The talented performer pranced and talked and sang with boundless energy and, while very funny at times, we found her monologue scatological and, for us, too filled with bawdy sexual material. It was difficult for us to understand why there was so much emphasis on sex in the performance.

There are issues in the lesbian world that concern us, the seeming instability of relationships is one, although this seems to hold true for heterosexual people as well. The high rate of divorce bears this out, and maybe the scarcity of long-term relationships is due to today's mobility. No longer is it necessary to work at a relationship; people move on literally and figuratively, always searching for the next, hopefully better, situation.

This was not true in our younger days. When we were Louise's age, we were happily involved with husbands, children, our homes and our own activities. We were committed to our marriages and made things work. Now our children see our lives as having been narrow and deprived, however these were the lives we chose and enjoyed.

We wonder why so many women are strident about being lesbian through dress, manner and attitude. Younger lesbians seem to often go through an almost "militant" stage, which may include short hair, mannish dress and mannerisms, and a show-the-world attitude. Time seems to soften this and older lesbians don't seem so concerned with being visible all the time. Maybe this stage is kind of like being a teenager, one is trying to establish identity and confidence through outward appearance.

The natural desire of women to have children presents a huge dilemma for us. Neither of us believe in artificial insemination for any woman, lesbian or not, since it is against the natural order of life. To us, adoption would seem like a reasonable solution to lesbians wanting to parent, especially since there are so many unwanted children in the world.

Our contact with gay men and lesbians has been very positive, and our lives have been enriched by the people we have met. Both of us have worked with gay men and have found they are unusually thoughtful and helpful. When people speak derogatorily about lesbians and gays, we now counter with what we have learned. When they snigger, a simple question such as "Why do you laugh?" or "What seems so funny?" will usually be followed by dead silence. Hopefully they will think about how they offend.

MARSHA BUCK

## "Bi" Understanding

*I am a fifty-two-year-old recently retired educator living in Alaska. I am also a musician and play oboe in the local symphony. My daughters, a food microbiologist and a pastry chef, live in Oregon and North Carolina.*

Please picture me as an ordinary mom who wears sweats around the house, loves to garden, and has lots of bad hair days. I may be unusual in that I was a school administrator before I retired, but thankfully that is becoming less unusual for women. I have two incredibly fine daughters who now both label themselves "bisexual."

As I write this chapter, I am trying to accurately remember the feelings I had when my daughters told me they were bisexual. That is hard for me to do, because I see myself as a mother who loves her daughters unconditionally. I think some of my difficult feelings about my daughters' bisexuality have been shoved deep down inside me, for fear of not being totally supportive. On top of that, I stubbornly refuse to be oppressed in as many areas of life as possible. Fear and other negative thoughts feel oppressive to me. When I feel oppression, I get active and tackle the issues head on even though my insides (and often my outsides, too) tremble like jello. Over the years, I have learned to live with the trembling because it goes away in the course of advocacy. This is how I handled my feelings when my daughters told me about their bisexuality.

My oldest daughter, Lys, is now twenty-six. She came out to me almost four years ago when she was a college student working on her master's degree. Prior to that time, Lys had often talked with me about her best friend, a young man with whom she shared many interests and much time, and who eventually told her that he was gay. Along with her good friend, she began to learn more about what it meant to be gay or lesbian. While this was going on, I became gradually aware of silent, nagging, little fears within myself that Lys might be a lesbian. I felt that if she were a lesbian, she would never again be worthy of pride in the eyes of my parents and our extended family. And I felt like crying because I thought *she* would never be happy!

I was not prepared, however, for the news that she was bisexual! That possibility had never occurred to me, primarily because I knew so little about bisexuality. I felt astonished at her news rather than fearful as I had felt earlier. My first reaction was to read books about bisexuality, and Lys was able to send me one book. Beyond that, I found one other book easily and then the search became difficult. I became frustrated that more books about bisexuality were not available. How were parents supposed to learn anything?

In her normal style and approach to life, Lys was then and is now confident about her sexuality. She had done her emotional and intellectual homework before she came out and has been "at home" with herself ever since. She expects other people to accept her with the same positive regard that she has for herself, and it appears to me that they do. I think it was her attitude of certainty and acceptance of bisexuality that kept me from dwelling on the myths about bisexuals. Many people think about bisexuals as people who need partners of both genders to be satisfied, as people who are oversexed, as people who are confused or just going through a phase on the way to either heterosexuality or homosexuality. I just dismissed these ideas as old myths that no one believed any more—after all, the myths didn't fit Lys! It makes me want to start a campaign to clear up the misinformation!

My biggest initial concerns were that Lys would not have children of her own, and that she would face job discrimination. I thoroughly enjoyed having children. I have always wanted my daughters to know that experience as well. And I am ready to be a grandma! Lys assured me right away that she planned on having a child of her own—that being bisexual and being a mother were not incompatible. As for my second concern, Lys has not experienced any job discrimination to date, and I plan to do my part in lobbying for passage of the Employment Non-Discrimination Act (ENDA) now before Congress to make certain that never happens.

Although I was full of questions and images of possible "weird" relationships when Lys announced her bisexuality, it appears that I may not have experienced as much anguish as some other parents. Part of the reason my struggle was not terribly intense or extended was that I participate in a women's support group. The women in the group have become great friends and colleagues, and most of them happen to be lesbian. With the support of friends like these, a daughter like Lys, and a relatively liberal mindset of my own, it didn't take long to think of myself as the proud mother of a bisexual daughter.

Lys kept educating me gradually during the first few years after she came out and kept cleaning up my language to make it more correct. When I would use the shortcut word "homosexual" to refer to "gay, lesbian, and bisexual" she would remind me that "homo" meant "one" and therefore was not appropriate for bisexuals. When I would call her bisexuality a "gender orientation" or a "sexual preference" she would remind me that it was her "sexual orientation."

Lys called one day to tell me that her friend, Dave, whom I had met and enjoyed, was a transsexual and was about to begin the process of becoming a woman, of becoming Dianne. This news threw me into a "tizzie"! How many more things were there to learn about sexual and gender differences? How far could I stretch emotionally while being a totally supportive mother? I wanted to close my mind and heart, but of course I didn't because that didn't fit my self image. Instead I invited Dave, who by this time had just become Dianne, to come and spend time in our home over the holidays. She came and we all had a wonderful time helping her learn some of the practical skills she needed in order to approach life as a woman. Getting to know Dianne as a loving, caring person was the best way I knew to deal with my desire to shut down my caring—and it worked.

I am continually becoming more aware of how many stereotypes and myths exist about bisexuals. One of the questions sometimes asked about bisexuals that fits into the stereotype category is whether bisexuals form long-term, committed, monogamous relationships. Lys and her partner of three years, Liz (who tells me openly that she likes her mother-in-law), definitely answer that question in the positive!

Shortly before Christmas a year ago, I received a second set of news for which I wasn't prepared. My twenty-three-year-old daughter, Lene, called to tell me that she was in love with a woman. This time my reaction was more emotional. Lene had been actively involved in loving relationships with men prior to this time. She is glamorous and shapely, and she clearly enjoys and returns the attentions of males in her day-to-day life. She came out explaining that I had taught and modeled open-mindedness while she was growing up. As a result, when she saw how happy her sister was in her relationship with Liz, she realized that she did not need to limit her loving only to men. She laughingly reported that her "gayness" was therefore *my* fault and thanked me profusely for it.

I had more difficulty dealing with Lene's coming out than I did with Lys'. In retrospect I think that after Lys came out, I shifted a large portion of my hopes and dreams for a "normal," formal wedding, daughter/son-in-law/grand-children ideal onto Lene. Those hopes and dreams seemed to be blown away by Lene's coming out. I felt depressed. I talked with friends to help sort out my feelings. I panicked at the thought of my parents finding out that *both* my daughters were bisexual. Would they be judgmental and distant?

Lene was not interested initially in putting the label of "bisexual" on herself. She felt that the important point was her love for Michelene and that a label wasn't needed. She was comfortable with calling herself gay, but knew that term referred primarily to men. Over time, I noticed in our conversations that she came to refer to herself as "bi."

When Lene first came out, Lys was not totally happy with the announcement. She feared that Lene was experimenting with a woman just for sexual excitement and that bisexuality had nothing to do with it. In addition, the unique niche that she had carved out for herself in our family now had to be shared. Over time, Lys' feelings changed. Lys has come to fully accept that Lene, too, is bisexual. She has seen that Lene is serious about working on a relationship with a woman.

Lys and Lene are two distinctly different bisexuals. Lys is in a long-term relationship with a woman and has experienced sexual attraction to men. Lene has been active in relationships with both men and a woman. Both daughters fit the definition of bisexuality which is the capacity for physical, romantic and/or emotional attraction to persons of both genders. Lene has experienced the pain of being shunned by lesbians because she "couldn't make up her mind" and "had the nerve to enjoy being with a man." Lys has experienced being part of a college association for gay, lesbian, and bisexual persons where bi's were not only welcomed but were often leaders. Both women, however, look toward the future with the "heart" knowledge that they can and will love people, not because of their gender or race or body build or social status, but because of the richness of the people themselves.

Not long ago, a friend of mine let me know that she loved my daughters, but thought they had made a "bad decision" by labeling themselves bisexual. I was sad that my friend felt that way and I was also filled with questions. Was it a decision for my daughters? Was it a choice? Much literature I have read emphasizes that psychologists do not consider sexual orientation to be a conscious choice for most people—a choice that can be voluntarily changed. When I asked my daughters how they felt, Lys replied that for her the choice was to acknowledge her bisexuality or to stay closeted. She has chosen not to deny who she is—not to live a lie. Lene replied that for her the choice was to be close-minded or open-minded enough to see the beauty in women as well as in men. She has chosen to see the possibility of loving either a woman or a man. Both responses were helpful although neither was an answer to the questions raised by my friend's comment. I still do not know if bisexuality was a decision or a choice for either Lys or Lene. At the moment, I'm feeling comfortable without an answer in light of Lys' recent comment to me, "Does it really matter?"

Most days I feel like an ordinary mom, but I also feel like a mom who is beginning to pull together many new thoughts about bisexuality. I don't think that there are as few parents of bisexuals or as few bisexual persons as it appears. I *do* think that many, many (perhaps even most) people experience physical, romantic and/or emotional attractions to persons of both genders, but our present culture has taught us to legitimize only the heterosexual side of those experiences. Within the gay and lesbian community, there is pressure to recognize only the homosexual side of those experiences. Therefore, many people who label themselves as straight, gay, or lesbian could more correctly fit the definition of bisexual.

I also think that many people feel confused about bisexuality because our lives are often given order by thinking in terms of black and white, right and left, yes and no, rather than gray and center and maybe. It is not easy for any of us, no matter how ordinary or extraordinary, to live with the full complexity that life really hands us!

BY JANE ALLEN

# The Silt of a River

*I was born in Peoria, Illinois in 1938. I am a psychotherapist, and interested in theater writing, quilting and gardening. I was divorced in 1975 after twenty years of marriage.*

My daughters are lesbians. I feel good that:

My children are happy and productive people.

Their friends and lovers are also appealing and vibrant people who have added greatly to my life.

They will have children if they choose.

They have been able to talk to me about their choices in life.

I have not lost my connection to them because of their decision to be gay.

I am sad that:

Some people would not like or even get to know my children because they are gay.

Occasionally a person will say something rude or cruel to my daughters and think this is justifiable because they are gay.

One day at a beach someone threw a bottle at one of my daughters and yelled "dyke."

At times, both they and I are fearful that we will be rejected or cause pain when we talk to friends or relatives about their lifestyle.

I have three bright and beautiful daughters. For a while, all three were lesbians. I have certainly had to think about many issues concerning homosexuality. My reactions have been multilayered, like the silt of a river laid down after each spring's flooding. In a way, we have been very lucky and our story must be easy compared to some. We each live in cities which have visible feminist and lesbian groups, and therefore each of us has a sense of community and support from other women. Still, there have been great difficulties.

My reactions have varied greatly. Sometimes I have seen their choice as positive: empowering them both personally and politically, raising their standards for developing their professional and personal lives, bringing really nice women into our lives, and connecting them to an exciting and dynamic community.

On the negative side has been: fear for their well-being and safety, concern about not having grandchildren, having to deal with some peoples' disapproval of them for the first time in my life, facing hurt and anger from their dad, and wondering at times if I had done something wrong in my parenting of them.

It's hard work to be the parent of lesbian children because you end up facing homophobia—both directly and through the experiences of your child. Once when we were traveling, we entered a full restaurant in an unfamiliar place in the Midwest. A silence fell, and people stared at us, I thought, with hostility. Fear seized me—would there be some sort of abuse? Verbal or even physical? Gay people can get hurt; it happens all the time. Was this going to be one of those times? Fortunately, it wasn't.

Until recently my own knowledge of homosexuality was very limited. Growing up in the forties in the Midwest, I knew no gay people. I do remember when I was fourteen, my mother said we should stop holding hands when we walked down the street because a friend of hers had teased her and said we looked strange. She didn't explain exactly what the concern was, but I understood that adult women weren't supposed to be publicly affectionate or something bad would happen.

During those years, my life was strongly influenced by my mother and my two grandmothers. My grandmothers had both been widowed and finished raising their families alone.

My mother and father had divorced when I was about four years old. My mom worked as a nurse and supported us. Each of these three women was dynamic and influenced me in her own way. One grandmother was an earth-mother, the other stood for social justice and love of nature. My mother was a professional woman.

After my Midwestern upbringing in the forties, I lived in the San Jose and San Francisco areas in the fifties and sixties. My children grew up in the civil rights and anti-war atmosphere of Berkeley. During that period, I knew two gay people. One of my supervisors lived with her female partner. She was very well-liked and accepted by others as far as I could tell. Also, when I worked part-time as a cashier in a restaurant near campus, one of the cooks was gay. He would talk about his male partner in much the same way as I talked about my husband. I rather liked this and found it easy to relate to him.

As my daughters were growing up in Berkeley and Davis, we were a typical happy family. Their dad finished grad school and was on the University of California faculty. Our kids were so appealing that other people would comment that they would consider having children themselves if they could be as nice as ours. Our oldest daughter loved animals, Nancy Drew mysteries and, later, dramatic arts. The middle daughter was energetic, sociable and very athletic. The youngest was an elfin guru, wise beyond her years and very witty. In high school and afterwards, they all had boyfriends and relationships with men. The oldest married and had two children.

During my daughters' late teens, their father and I divorced and this was a difficult time for them. The issues were complex and included many differences of style in personal relationships and politics. Like many women, I had at least partially deferred my professional and individual development as I focused on being a wife and mother. I found that in my thirties I wanted it all—to go to college, be more intimate with my husband, *and* have personal freedom. We had many arguments about feminism, which I saw as a request to share more of our lives, including the tasks at home. He saw this as a ploy to make him do more housework, or as a kind of rejection.

Sometimes we fought. Sometimes we were depressed. The girls' adolescence was not as tranquil as it might have been. It seemed as though their father and I were going through our own adolescence. Did we disillusion them about male/female relationships? I don't know.

Our marriage collapsed for good when our oldest daughter was in college. The other girls seemed college-bound and had pretty active lives in every respect. During this period, my oldest daughter had a very home-and-family oriented lifestyle, while the youngest went to Southeast Asia as an exchange student. My middle daughter became involved in a women's health collective which provided health care services in our town.

The first to come out was my middle daughter and it was a gradual process. She met and worked with many women—including gay women. I met some of them and thought they were very nice, socially committed and responsible people. She had expressed a feeling that women were more emotionally developed than men. She was living with two lesbian housemates and I wasn't particularly surprised when she said that she had become lovers with one of them. She was already part of a community of women and I wasn't worried about her current situation because she seemed to have a lot of support in her decision and she seemed happy.

Prior to this, she had been involved with a young man in college. They planned to be married, but they couldn't seem to agree on how to be parents. He was traditional, expecting her to be the primary parent. She wanted a more equal division of responsibility. Eventually they separated.

She was considering training to become a midwife during this time, and their separation seemed to help her focus more on her career. Her woman lover was supportive of both her personal and professional goals. Emotionally, financially and in the division of tasks, she supported my daughter's ideas and growth. There wasn't the sense of struggle—or the fear that the roles of wife and mother would take away the chance for other things to develop. This daughter is now in medical school and is involved with a young man whom she may marry.

My oldest daughter came out a year and a half later. She had gone from a very active social and academic life early in her college career and marriage to a very inward-looking period after the birth of her children. It was hard to get her out of the house.

I was concerned about her development and wondered if she was happy. Her children, a girl and a boy, darling and bright, seemed to flourish. Her husband was gone a lot, studying to be a lawyer. As she began to expand her life again, she got involved in women's action groups, like NOW, and began taking martial arts. She was happy in the company of women and really seemed to blossom. She told me that part of feeling good about herself included advancing the cause of women. She was particularly enthusiastic about women holding political office and felt as though she wanted to work toward the goal of women having equal opportunity in every way.

She and her husband are now separated and share time equally with the children. She has finished her undergraduate degree and is working and applying to graduate schools. Her partner, a graduate student in political science, is also involved in parenting the children. I was more surprised about her decision to be involved with women, but I love her as I always have.

Within the same year, my youngest daughter, now a college student, told me that she was also gay. I had wondered many years before if she might make that decision. Her relationships with men seemed a bit off. She never really "fell in love," and kept telling me, "Mom, I just seem to keep breaking men's hearts!"

I hope they each felt my love for them during these transitions. However, with my third daughter's coming out, I must admit I feared other people's reaction to our family. At this time, my ex-husband asked to talk to me about it. He was very angry with me, thinking that I had ruined our daughters. I remembered with guilt a debate I had many years before with his therapist, a woman, about the children's independence and their learning to do things like change their own bicycle tires. She said I was going to raise daughters that no man would want to live with. In my own heart, I didn't think they were ruined, or that I had done anything to them. Their dad was upset and angry but, to his credit, he has been able to maintain contact with them and loves them even though he strongly disapproves of their lifestyles. It has been a while now, and he is probably closer to his daughters than he ever has been. Everyone has weathered the storm of feelings. I am very proud of them.

We have passed through many stages as a family: surprise, fear, guilt, anger—and I feel these things again at times. But we finally moved on to acceptance and just wanting to get on with life and enjoy it. I rarely worry if my daughters' lesbianism is a stage, or a political statement, or my fault. I am still wading through my own stereotypes about lesbians. A mixed bag indeed, including that they are particular bearers of women's culture, easier to work with politically, harder to work with politically, have fewer problems in relationships, close out straight people.... Fortunately I meet enough gay women now so that I must abandon one after another of these ideas.

Recently my youngest daughter and I were on a vacation in the Midwest. We happened to be in Chicago during a Gay Pride parade. There was one group of parents of gays who carried signs which said, "Yes, her mother does know," and "We love our gay children." I was so glad to see them and felt that I knew and shared some of the journey that had brought them to march in that parade.

by Ginger and Katheryn

## Our Separate Lives

*Ginger and Katheryn are pseudonyms for two Asian-American women living in a large city in California. Their daughters are friends. This interview was conducted at Ginger's inner city house in September 1986.*

*Louise Rafkin:* How did you find out that your daughters were lesbians?

*Ginger:* I don't think I really "found out"; she lives her own life. She was engaged and then she said she wasn't going to get married.

*LR:* Did she say she was involved with women?

*Ginger:* Not right out.

*LR:* And for you, Katheryn?

*Katheryn:* Well, my daughter was living with a man. She called me and told me she was going to stop living with the man, and start living with a woman. Then she told me she was a lesbian. Now, how were my feelings at that time? I don't know if it has anything to do with it, but having only one child, I think, made a difference. I got used to it, though.

*LR:* How did you feel, were you shocked? Had you known any lesbians?

*Katheryn:* Of course I was shocked. I just never suspected that she would turn around and be a lesbian.

*LR:* Did you talk with anyone about it?

*Katheryn:* No. I just kept it to myself. I did tell my husband though. He is not one to express his feelings too much, but he certainly did not like it. He said to me, "But what can you do about it?" So we let her live her own life.

*LR:* Because she was your only child, did you feel a loss about not having grandchildren?

*Katheryn:* That was on my mind, but that's the life she wants to live. I have resolved myself to never being a mother-in-law, never a grandmother. What can you do?

*LR:* Did you have any ideas about what a lesbian was?

*Katheryn:* I knew of lesbians, but didn't know any personally.

*Ginger:* I read about things in the paper. And I think it has been going on for generations. I think everyone should live their own life. It really doesn't bother me how my children live. She always brings her friends home, for parties and dinners.

*LR:* What about your communities, or your families and extended families? Does anyone else know that you have lesbian daughters?

*Ginger:* Our relatives are not that close.

*Katheryn:* As far as my relatives go, if they do know they haven't discussed that with me. It's probably something they know but don't discuss. I don't know if my daughter has discussed it with them.

*LR:* Do you know your daughters' friends, or find them any different from heterosexual women?

*Ginger:* Most of them are professional. I just consider them her friends.

*Katheryn:* That's how I feel.

* * *

*LR:* Can you talk about the fear you have about being identified in this book, not that I don't think it's a valid concern...

*Katheryn:* You say fear. There is no fear. We just want to live our own lives and we want our daughters to live their own lives. Not to exploit them or advertise them.

*LR:* You are not worried about your friends finding out about it?

*Ginger:* Not at all.

*Katheryn:* But it would be best if my husband and I kept a low profile about it.

*LR:* Because of society's feelings about homosexuality?

*Katheryn:* It has nothing to do with how society feels.

*Ginger:* My daughter left home at eighteen or twenty. We have lived our separate lives for a long time.

*Katheryn:* Do you think that lesbians should be advertised, that the parents should be involved in it?

*LR:* No, but I know with my own mother, there was a lot of fear on her part about what others would say about her. People may feel that it's the parents' "fault" and condemn them. Recently, I went to my high school reunion and I came out to many of my old friends. There hasn't been any backlash about this, at least to her, but it's a small town and people do talk. I can understand her fear—it's something *we* live with every day.

*Ginger:* I don't think that kind of talking happens so much in the big cities.

*Katheryn:* I think that as long as there are humans, there are two types, those who will talk and those who are open-minded. The way I feel about it is that if they know, fine; if they don't, I leave well enough alone.

*LR:* It sounds like you are very accepting in terms of saying you live your lives and they live their lives. Do you think there are cultural opinions or attitudes that have helped you to feel this way?

*Katheryn:* It just dawned on me that Ginger and I only have one daughter each. We have to accept them as they are. I think you should also interview some mothers who have more than one daughter.

*LR:* It seems like it can go either way. There are those women who have one daughter who say, "This is my only daughter; I want her to be a certain way," and those who say, "This is my only daughter and we are family no matter what happens."

*Ginger:* How can they say their daughter has to be a certain way? You can't change it.

*LR:* People try.

*Katheryn:* I think Asians have different backgrounds, different feelings, and different traditions than others do. They are different than American people, from Chicanos, etc. Having only one daughter, you have to accept how they live their lives.

*Ginger:* If you had two daughters, you perhaps would compare them. But that is not my problem. All my children are very independent.

*LR:* Have you ever thought you might like to talk to other mothers who have lesbian daughters?

*Ginger:* Really, we don't talk about our children that much to other people. Everybody I know has several children; we don't want to hear about their children, and they don't want to hear everything about ours!

*Katheryn:* I don't feel that way, as far as hearing about their children and vice versa. However, my husband and I don't talk about that part of her life. We don't say she is lesbian, or she is straight.

*Ginger:* We just say she is working...she comes over for dinner.... We always welcome her friends here, in fact we have gone on trips with them. I don't say that my son is heterosexual.

*LR:* So you talk to your friends about them, but don't mention who they are living with, or going with...

*Katheryn:* That's right. Nobody is going to turn around and ask us that, because I would turn around and tell them it is none of their business to ask such things. My friends, they'll know what to ask and that's not something they would ask. I don't think the relatives know, they might suspect it, but I would rather have it that way.

*LR:* Because you want her to tell them if she wants to?

*Katheryn:* What do you gain from it?

*Ginger:* Our friends are not really her friends; there is a generation gap.

*LR:* You don't think they would have the same feelings about her if they knew?

*Katheryn:* They wouldn't have the same feelings for us if they knew.

*LR:* Why? What would they think?

*Ginger:* …I don't know, we don't really have friends who are so inquisitive.

*LR:* And your closest friends?

*Katheryn:* My closest friend does not even suspect it.

*LR:* But what would you think they would feel about you?

*Katheryn:* I don't know. You never ask them, "How do you feel now that you know my daughter is a lesbian?" Would you turn around and ask somebody that?

*LR:* Well, my mother went to her best friend and talked with her when she found out about me.

*Ginger:* Our friends, both my husband's and mine, are not that close.

*LR:* How does your husband feel about her?

*Ginger:* She is the apple of his eye.

*LR:* Do either of you have questions you would like to ask me?

*Ginger:* What's the difference between lesbian and feminist?

*LR:* Feminism has to do with politics and fighting for women's rights and equality. Many women feel that lesbianism is something they are born with, and some women feel that lesbianism can come about through being feminist.

*Ginger:* So a feminist is not necessarily a lesbian.

*LR:* And a lesbian is not necessarily a feminist.

*Before the tape started, Ginger and Katheryn both wanted to be assured that there would be no way of anyone finding out their identities and the identities of their daughters. Ginger's daughter, Lotus, overheard the conversation and was upset by the degree to which Ginger and Katheryn were "in the closet." Before leaving the house, she expressed her disappointment to them.*

*Katheryn:* How do you feel about what Lotus said, that she felt sorry for us because of our concern. She was quite disturbed. Why?

*LR:* I don't know exactly what she was feeling. But I was very upset when I felt like my mother was ashamed about what I was, wasn't proud of who I was.

*Katheryn:* Of course we are proud of who she is, but not the life that she leads. That is separate.

*LR:* I think for Lotus, and for me, it is the same. Who we are and the lives that we live are the same.

*Katheryn:* So in other words, you think if you are a lesbian then you should advertise it and everybody should know, including the parents' friends. The way she sounded, she said that she was sorry for us that we couldn't accept her as what she is. We accept it, but we don't have to advertise it.

*LR:* If you accept her lesbianism but don't acknowledge it, you cut out a whole part of her life. I don't know your daughter's life, but with many women, their activities, their politics and involvement with the gay community is part of their life. I recently won a writing award for my writing in a gay paper. I would like my mother to be able to say that and feel as good about it as I do. Through not talking about it, it somehow feels as though people are ashamed. Maybe that is what Lotus was feeling.

*Katheryn:* There are certain rebuttals. You're proud, you have said that is what you are. But as far as being a parent is concerned, we don't fully accept our children as lesbians and have to advertise it. Let's say it is bad enough to have a child who is a lesbian, but to turn around and advertise it to the whole world...and to your best friends and all that...that's another thing.

*LR:* If we all didn't think it was bad on some level, then it wouldn't be such an issue. What Lotus was saying about being in the book wouldn't be difficult for you. But it is still not a world where it is okay to be homosexual.

*Ginger:* We accept it, like we accept other things in the world. I accept life as it comes.

*Katheryn:* But it is not okay...I accept her as a lesbian because she is my daughter. But telling my friends, that is something else...I would prefer if it were different.

*Ginger:* Grandchildren!

*Katheryn:* What other people do is the norm, and I don't consider being a lesbian the norm. But I wouldn't fight it, or change it, or convert her...

*LR:* You might find it difficult...

*Katheryn:* There are lesbians who went back straight; there are people who change. Just because you are still a lesbian doesn't mean it can't happen. You say it's difficult but it happens...

*LR:* I agree, but I think it may be difficult for you to change her...

*Ginger:* It would be only by her own free will.

\* \* \*

*Katheryn:* Do you find it traumatic to interview parents like this?

LR: Yes, very.

*Katheryn:* Because you fear what's going to happen—emotionally?

*LR:* Yes, and because I think it's very hard to ask people you have never met before about their feelings. I think each of the women I have interviewed is very brave to allow a stranger to ask such personal questions.

MARIA GARCIA

## Of Prejudice and Acceptance

*I'm Latina, a single parent, with two daughters. I'm fifty-six years old and work as a clerk in a large office building. I am a practicing Catholic and a lector and Eucharistic minister in my church.*

My oldest daughter, Carrie, told me she was a lesbian when she was eighteen. At the time I was very upset. It was such a new idea. I had always thought I was liberal and had always lived around gay people in San Francisco's Mission district. Some of my neighbors were gay and I had always respected their choices.

As I am a practicing Catholic, I went to see my priest and told him I felt very depressed after Carrie told me about her lesbianism. My priest suggested that I go to a Parents and Friends of Lesbians and Gays meeting, and I did. I saw that all parents go through similar feelings when they find out their children are lesbian or gay. I began attending the meetings and have been a member for the last four years. I have found that it is all right to love Carrie, but first it was important to understand her life. I really feel that through this organization, and through verbalizing with other parents and reading literature, my daughter and I have become much closer because of my accepting attitude. I have met many fine lesbians and feel quite comfortable with the situation as it is.

For some time, however, I thought that perhaps Carrie was a lesbian because I had sent her to Catholic school and she hadn't had enough exposure to boys her own age. I'm a single parent and my children only saw their father on the weekends, though we had men friends and she has close relationships with her uncles. I thought that perhaps if she had grown up with a male in the house, things would have been different. But I have never met anyone I wanted to be involved with. I also wondered if I had been too strict and if

I hadn't been home enough for her. I felt this guilt. I got over it by analyzing these fears and finding that they were unfounded. I now believe people are gay because they are born that way. Almost every gay person I have met through the parents' group has said that they knew at a very early age they were gay. It's not something you wake up with one day and decide, "Oh, today I think I'll be a lesbian!"

My daughter lives near enough to me to be able to come over and visit. If there is someone she is terribly fond of, she'll bring her for dinner. There isn't any animosity between us, and she has a good relationship with her younger sister. I work within the Catholic church to improve relations with the gay community, including work with the nuns and priests. Currently, I am involved in a group that works closely with the Archbishop. It's a slow process and more education is needed.

I told my older sister, Carrie's godmother, about Carrie's lesbianism and she is very accepting. She loves Carrie as she is. I haven't told anyone else in my family, because I feel it is for Carrie to tell them. She respects my privacy and she doesn't go around saying, "My mother's heterosexual and celibate." So why should I go around telling people she is a lesbian? I think that is in poor taste. People should be allowed the privacy of choice, of telling who they want.

There are so many people with anti-gay and anti-lesbian feelings. When the topic comes up, I will say something about gay people if I feel that saying something will make a difference. If I see that it won't change people's feelings, I just let the subject drop. There are gay people in the office where I work. In my department there is a gay man who is liked by all, and people don't say anything bad about him, but will say something about other gays. I talk with him about his gayness, and he knows my daughter. He ran into her at a gay dance and asked her if I knew about her lesbianism, and she told him that I accepted her. He and I now have a closer relationship; we talk and stop for drinks. We've always been friends, but there is a closer affinity with someone who is really understanding and accepting.

I was also told about a woman at work who is gay, so I made a special effort to get to know her. Once she let her defenses down, I found her to be warm and friendly. She was hardworking and helped me in several projects. A different woman at work asked me if I knew that the woman was gay. I told her that I had always found her pleasant to work with and that her sexual preference had never once come up in our working relationship. I hope that made her think.

Being Mexican-American, I am part of a minority group. Many people have a lot of ill-feeling towards us—that we are lazy, or stupid, or other stereotypes. Although I don't hear much of it here in San Francisco, I understand what prejudice can feel like.

This is America and people should have a choice. I am a Catholic and would not have an abortion, but that doesn't mean other people have to feel the same way I do. The government does not have a right to interfere with one's private life. It disturbs me, but it happens. I watch television and listen to radio programs about these issues and I hear people say very strong anti-Semitic, anti-gay, anti-Catholic things that are extremely prejudiced. I find it frightening. It's almost the mentality of the time of Hitler. I grew up listening to this kind of prejudice and propaganda and it disturbs me greatly.

I believe you have to accept your children as they are. The more contact that parents have with the gay community, the better relationship they will have with their children. By isolating themselves from their children, they can't move to understanding homosexuality. I think it's most important to read about it, and there is literature all over about it—even in the Catholic bookstores.

And I want information from Carrie that will cement our relationship. A close family is part of my heritage. I came from a family of five and my family means a lot to me. I don't want to do anything to damage my very close and intimate relationship with either of my children. They are very honest and open with me. I give them my opinions and if they don't like them they can tell me. I really love my children. I want to help them live through any miserable periods of their lives, to share in their happiness, to be there for them.

DEBORAH

# The Odd Man Out

*I'm forty-six, a cardiology technician, divorced and I live in suburban New Jersey. I am in the process of moving one hour from my work so that I can live next door to my daughter, Melissa, who is twenty-four.*

Until Melissa came along, I had never thought about lesbians. I don't think I knew any gay people, and I certainly did not suspect that Melissa was gay. Ironically, I now know there are several gay people in our family, including my cousin, Massachusetts State Representative Barney Frank.

As a teenager, Melissa was popular and beautiful and went out with a zillion boys. In eighth grade, she and her boyfriend were picked as "class couple." Sometime in her fifteenth year, I separated from her father. When we finally divorced, Melissa took it hard. She was hospitalized with a nervous break down. Subsequently, she left high school.

When Melissa was sixteen, I started to notice how much she talked about a certain friend of hers. I noticed that she ignored her boyfriend in order to spend time with this friend. I joked with her that she might be gay, but basically I just thought she was behaving strangely. Melissa assured me that she wasn't gay.

When Melissa was eighteen, she developed an obsession about the TV program *Cagney and Lacey*. She had a thing for Cagney, the blond one, though throughout this time she was still dating boys. During an episode, she turned to me and asked me if I thought she was gay, and I guess I said yes. I suggested that she go to find a group of people to talk to, and she went to the library to "read up." At the library, she found that the books on homosexuality were locked inside a cabinet. She told me that inside one of the books, she found a slip of paper saying: "You are not alone." There was also a number for a gay and lesbian teen group. She called the number and that night told us she was gay.

At first I tried to be supportive, but then reality hit. Soon she came home with the first woman she went out with. I felt tense and angry and was quite nasty and short tempered with her. I knew this was bad behavior, but I couldn't stop myself. I didn't feel guilty because I was so mad at her. During this time I didn't have my husband's support, and Melissa and I fought constantly. Everything was changing and I didn't know what was happening. I started therapy. At that point Melissa wasn't even speaking to her father. Things were very bad.

Melissa told my parents right away and also my in-laws. I knew that telling other people was okay and was the right thing to do, but I didn't want to. I tried going to PFLAG meetings, but the meetings were too dramatic for me. I just didn't feel comfortable with the parents who cried, or brought religion into the picture. I felt guilty because those in charge of the meeting seemed so accepting and I just wasn't there yet.

I saw that Melissa was happy. But she was also changing. She started looking totally different. Out went the hair dye and make-up. Essentially, she stopped dressing for boys. I missed the other Melissa, because that's the one I knew. We could still shop and do things together, but something had changed. Still, I tried to support her. Mentally she seemed much stronger and although she had some bad relation-ships, she was trying. I made a decision to stand behind her and offer my love.

This was seven years ago, and I love the Melissa that I know now. She is twenty-five, a confident college graduate, a pre-school teacher, a very beautiful human being. Missy came out to her boss and co-workers and they all accepted her; I thought she was very brave. I adore her lover, Martha, another wonderful woman. But I still can't help wishing that Melissa had hooked up with a man. Being a lesbian makes her life more difficult and that makes me sad.

My best friend knows about Melissa and everything is fine with her. I feel ashamed about not telling anyone else; I have never told any of my other friends or co-workers. They are not a very liberal group and I don't want to put up with their talking behind my back, or pitying me, or treating Melissa differently. I don't feel good about it, but I just can't face them. I'm too afraid of their judgments and their ideas.

For people who don't know, I've made up a story about Melissa living with a boyfriend. It's difficult not being able to talk with them about the normal things about Melissa's life, but I think it would be harder to know they were not being very kind about her. Even my parents feel badly that Missy will never marry a man, though I believe they love her as much as they did before.

Both my children were raised the same, and my son is heterosexual. Sometimes I have the feeling that Melissa's lesbianism is due to her bad relationship with her father. However they are now close again. Melissa was always well liked by both girls and boys. Even when she was in kindergarten, I had to go to the principal to get the boys to leave her alone! When we talk about childhood and her crushes on various girls, I realize she kept many of her feelings to herself. I feel badly that we couldn't talk when she was growing up. If I were to do it all over again, I would somehow show her that there are many possibilities for intimate relationships.

I am moving to a different area to be closer to Melissa. I am leaving my middle-class wealthy neighborhood to be in Melissa's life because we want to be closer and she doesn't feel comfortable where I live. She lives in a mixed suburban area with a college nearby.

I have to say I'm still uncomfortable with the whole lesbian thing, and I feel even more uncomfortable around gay men. We talk about everything, but Melissa is right when she tells me to "deal" with my feelings about her life. All of Melissa's friends are gay. They look and act very feminine, which is easier for me than if they were "butch." Though I am with them all the time, and they are a wonderful group of women, it still feels strange. I feel out of place. My life is not like theirs. Their experiences are different, and I feel like the odd man out. I guess that is how she feels in my world.

ANN "LANDAU" DAWSON

# Yom Kippur

*I'm an older Jewish mother of five and grandmother. I have always been a progressive feminist and activist. Now retired, I'm free for full-time volunteer work. Much of my activities are with the Berkeley group of Parents and Friends of Lesbians and Gays.*

I was asked once why I gave such high priority to my work in Parents and Friends of Lesbians and Gays. I thought of Yom Kippur, one of the most important Jewish holidays, the annual Day of Atonement. Yom Kippur came about because, as a people, we think ourselves guilty for the Jews who accepted conversion during the Spanish Inquisition. It was an early version of social responsibility.

Twenty-two years ago, a darling daughter confided—with confusion and fear—her sexual orientation to me. At that time, I was full of misconceptions and corrupted values. Instead of helping her, I increased her pain by saying, "Yes, you're sick, we must get you some therapy." Good heavens! It was our society, including myself, that was sick. Because I let her down then, she had to struggle all alone. It was no thanks to her doctor or myself that she finally won out to a healthy acceptance of herself.

Perhaps in helping today's young lesbians and gays and their parents, I am doing a kind of atonement. My daughter forgave me long ago, and I try not to waste energy on guilt. Responsibility, though, is something else. I do believe the saying, "If you are not part of the solution, you are part of the problem."

The problems homosexuals faced were even worse when my daughter came out to me than they are now. Persecution of gays and lesbians was more intense. It was a felony to commit a homosexual act. The most liberal medical viewpoint was that is was an aberration, a sexual preference

84

caused by childhood trauma. Accepting that diagnosis, my daughter struggled against her orientation for years. She had psychiatric "help" and even married. Of course, neither the psychiatry or marriage worked. But she tried for a long time to change herself.

My daughter was a third generation political activist. In the 1960s and early '70s, even progressive political movements didn't accept homosexuals. That seems inconceivable now, but then the peace movement, and even the women's liberation movement, didn't have openly homosexual members. Of course, at least ten percent of the activists must have been lesbian or gay but they had to be in the closet. Thank goodness my daughter was strong enough to come through those dark ages to healthy self-acceptance.

With time, I too attained a realistic viewpoint about lesbianism. Once I realized she wasn't sick, that her orientation was normal, the hardest thing to accept was that she probably wouldn't have children. The year she was born, 1945, we began to learn of the mass extermination of Jews by the Nazis. Our whole family, outside the few in the United States, had been slaughtered. The thought that my beautiful, intelligent daughter would not continue our family was difficult.

Also, I love being a mother. Of all the good things in my life—and it's been interesting and exciting in many ways—my relationship with my children has been perhaps the most rewarding. Even as a child, my lesbian daughter had always been "parental" and I'd assumed she would become a mother. I know she would have been a wonderful one. But when she was young, it was unheard of for lesbians to have children unless they stayed in the closet. What lousy alternatives! I'm bitter about my daughter and so many others of her generation being deprived of parenthood—and the world being deprived of the splendid kids they could have produced.

For quite a while, I didn't think of lesbian/gay liberation as a socio-political issue. I realize now I must have been very dense because I've always been active for the rights of other minorities and women. But it didn't dawn on me that the civil liberties movement should include homosexuals till the Briggs Initiative. This California initiative (which was defeated by a vote of fifty-eight percent to forty-two percent) would have amended the state's constitution to prevent homosexuals, or anyone who advocates acceptance of homosexuality as normal, from being employed in the public schools. It would have been impossible for homosexual students to get help from school counselors or for science teachers to tell their pupils the truth about homosexuality. It was a loud echo from the 1950s; the "red scare" and "loyalty oaths" imposed on teachers at that time. Only now, instead of "reds," the witch hunt would have been against homosexuals. I campaigned against the initiative, which did not pass. This work led me into working for Parents and Friends of Lesbians and Gays.

My other children accept their sister's orientation. They've always looked up to her. One said, "If she's a lesbian, then a lesbian is an okay thing to be." But my husband died not knowing she'd "reverted" to her orientation after her marriage. He believed, and *wanted* to believe, that it had all been an adolescent phase. He felt such guilt—thought it was a reflection on him as a father, as a man. He never could understand that women loving women doesn't mean they hate men. He never got past thinking that. My daughter protected him from knowing that her orientation was permanent. The child parented the parent. I've found that protective attitude toward parents is widespread among lesbians.

But it shouldn't be necessary. In PFLAG, we're working to help educate society to the fact that homosexuality is a normal, healthy orientation. My group is low-key, relaxed, supportive. Many parents newly aware of a child's orientation are upset and confused. The old myths are still pretty widespread. It helps to meet and talk freely with other parents who are accepting of their kids' gayness.

Such acceptance is sometimes hard to achieve. The first step is to get the garbage out of your head. If you have been conditioned to believe that heterosexuality is the only normal sexuality, and that any other orientation is at best sick, then finding your own child is lesbian or gay makes you feel like a bad parent, a parent who has somehow deformed your child. Parents who don't at first have some reactions like this are few. But mothers of blue-eyed or left-handed children don't feel guilty. Such people are in the minority, too, but there is not the social stigma attached to those traits. In PFLAG, we explain to terrified, confused, and guilty parents that homosexuality is no more a handicap than being blue-eyed; that nearly all the problems lesbians and gays face are from sick societal attitudes. For many, it's very helpful to hear this from other parents. And we do some surrogate parenting for lesbians and gays separated from their families, ideologically, or geographically, or both.

In our culture, sexuality is an important part of people's lives and ideally, parents should understand, accept and support their children as they are. The world has become less intolerant since my daughter was young, but still too many parents are homophobic. Too few are like one of the mothers in our group who says, "My daughter's orientation never bothered me. She's a loving person, and isn't that wonderful? Her capacity to love, not who she loves, is what's important."

If only someone had told me that when my daughter was eighteen. We would have both been spared a lot of grief.


*Editor's Note: In the first edition of this book, Ann used a pseudonym, not because she wasn't "out" as a mother of a lesbian, but to protect the identity of her daughter whose job situation was tricky. Ann died in 1992 and at the request of her daughter, Kip, her real name has been inserted in this edition.*

JANE FERGUSON

# No Magic Wand

*I have had a check-ered career as a teacher of English as a second language in Cameroon, Yugoslavia, and Willimantic, Connecticut, as a regular English teacher in a community college, a free-lance editor, and director/teacher of a program for teenage mothers. When asked at a job interview what my life goal was, I replied that it was to find a full-time job with a decent salary before I have to retire.*

Parenthood is a crazy-quilt at best, and the task of sorting out my feelings about being the mother of lesbians is a very tough one. There have been many dramatic moments in my relationships with my four children, many guilt trips, many disappointments, but the overall impression, when I look at that quilt, is of bright colors and exciting patterns. And when I think of the narrow, limited person, rigidly sure of all kinds of impossible standards, that I was and would still be were it not for my kids, I can't regret any of it.

I don't imagine many babies have been born whose parents had no agenda for them, for better or worse. First babies, in particular, usually arrive heavily burdened with expectations. I suspect that few parents, when presented with pink bundles by cooing nurses, have foreseen lesbianism as their daughters' sexual choice. I certainly was no exception, and while I think I can honestly say that I have accepted that choice on the part of both my daughters, I have to admit that I would wave a magic wand if I could and provide them with Prince Charmings, rose-covered cottages, and nuclear families, even in the face of all the statistics about divorce, wife-beating, and child abuse. This is where I came from, and what I have, perhaps ignorantly, imagined that I had in my own life. However, there is no magic wand, and my choice has been very clear: accept, learn, love.

My older daughter, Louisa, left home for good at seventeen, and after that there were several years when communication was very difficult. I always seemed to say, or at least suggest, the wrong thing. I don't think that had much, if anything, to do with sexual orientation; I'm sure it was just inevitable growing pains. But having felt very close to her during her early teens, I was really devastated by the change. She told us she was a lesbian when she was twenty, just when we were in crisis with our adoptive fifteen-year-old son. The combination of problems was pretty overwhelming—I felt terribly guilty, a total failure as a parent. I asked our pediatrician to recommend a psychiatrist. When I arrived for the first visit, he asked me what was bothering me. When I described the problems, and mentioned that two of our four children were adopted and black, he started visibly. Then he asked if I had ever considered the possibility that Louisa's lesbianism had been caused by our adoption of black kids. That was a guilt trip I hadn't yet taken, but I was certainly ready for another free ride!

Naturally, my husband and I have given a lot of thought to the question of *why* our daughters are lesbians. As a child and teenager, Louisa seemed to be headed for a "normal" heterosexual life, something that can't be said about our younger daughter, Lindsay, who is also choosing homosexual relationships, though without the intellectual element of feminism. Louisa had high school boyfriends; Lindsay has always had male friends and been involved in "boy's activities" almost exclusively, but the male friends don't seem to have been lovers. Her lovers are female, and what bothers us most is the fact that so far these relationships haven't been revealed to the other parents, who "would die" if they knew. In high school, Lindsay adopted a male persona, and many of her friends thought she was a boy named Bob. This phase passed, and we hope to live long enough to see her comfortable with herself, racially and sexually, and accepted by everyone she loves.

My oldest, Louisa, remembers my horrified reaction to the very idea of a lesbian relationship, when she was in her teens and someone mentioned the possibility of a daughter bringing home a female lover. I don't remember this, but it is probably true. Such a prospect was totally outside my thinking or imagining at that point. Since then, however, among other educational experiences, I have seen my widowed mother fall head over heels in love with another woman. I am now convinced that many, if not most, people have a variety of close relationships in the course of their lives, sometimes expressed physically, sometimes not, and that the sex of the loved one is secondary.

When Louisa came out, there was still a lot of edginess between us. I think I can say that my children's sex lives are something I've been able to stay away from, probably because I wasn't very comfortable about discussing sex with them, even though my own mother was very good at this touchy aspect of parenthood. I remember telling Louisa that I wasn't satisfied with her description of her new lover in a letter—"X and I are lovers!"—because that was literally all she said. We had not met the woman, and we wanted to know what she was like. I also remember being very upset when Lindsay went to visit her sister in Boston and was taken to a lesbian bar, at age twelve. I didn't think she should be taken to any bar at all, and I was certainly distressed when she came home bug-eyed about the women dancing together. I'm not a touchy-feely person, which goes with my Puritanism about discussing sex, and one aspect of the lesbian world which I have had a lot of trouble dealing with (as I do in the heterosexual world as well) is open displays of sexual affection.

One thing that has frequently struck me about Louisa's friends and her world is the generally high level of intelligence combined with a low level of formal education. Their eyes are bright, their minds are sharp, but they are heavily into superstition, the stars, reincarnation, their karma, most of them unacquainted with dear Brutus. When Louisa was nearly killed in a car accident (she thought it was her karma not to have accidents, and was careless), her friend flipped through a star book in the hospital trying to discover the "reason" for the disaster. I had to bite my tongue not to ask why she hadn't looked in the book beforehand. While I certainly recognize my own need to approach life and death from a poetic, metaphoric position in order to survive, I like to be able to argue and, hopefully, reason. With all their talent and brains, I wish that Louisa and her friends would work towards taking over the world—but on the whole, they are very apolitical, not seeming to realize that things could be much worse, and probably will be, if women don't take power instead of withdrawing from the world. I don't see a lot of difference between the old housebound or convent-bound place of women and this refusal to deal actively with the world as a whole.

One place where our feelings clashed painfully was over the issue of a women-only restaurant which Louisa and some friends operated for about a year. I would not eat in a place that wouldn't serve everyone, any more than I would join a club that wouldn't accept blacks or Jews. The idea of refusing to serve her own father and brothers really upset me. I had to concede that a comfortable "space" is nice, but I think it has to be really private. We thought of a lot of facetious names for the enterprise, none of which the owners found amusing; The Feminist Miss-Steak was our ultimate effort (the restaurant was vegetarian). However, the anti-male hostility of many lesbians is not something I can laugh off; it disturbs me very much, as does the anti-straight woman cold shoulder. I quit going to the local women's center a number of years ago because of the unwelcoming atmosphere there. I hope it has changed. I think sisterhood should be a lot more powerful than that. I am also very much disturbed by the practice of excluding male children of lesbian women from occasions such as music festivals, making them stay in a kind of detention center outside the grounds. I feel that is a form of violence against those children.

While I know that many lesbians (and straight women) have a nightmarish past of abuse by fathers and other males, I don't believe that eliminating males from their lives is the way to deal with that pain, nor is it the way to accomplish full human equality and respect.

The biggest and most painful issue that I have had to deal with as a mother of a lesbian was the conception of our granddaughter. Louisa had told us that she and an old friend, who was not her lover, had long talked of sharing parenthood. Louisa had even been to adoption meetings, investigating the possibility of single-parent adoption of a hard-to-place child. We were able to be very enthusiastic about that idea; we were well aware of the need for parents for children already in the world. But suddenly a bombshell: Louisa's friend Marguerite was pregnant, having used a turkey baster to inseminate herself with sperm donated by "an old friend." The father was grandly making this contribution to a human being he had no thought of being responsible for in any other way—indeed, I don't think he even knows of the child's birth. We were appalled, and even more so when we received the added piece of news that if the child was a boy, he would be given to someone who liked males! Having lost a baby myself, I doubted that this would actually occur, but the very suggestion sent shock waves through the family, especially among the male members, and we were all relieved when Teresa turned out to be a girl. We were also relieved that Louisa and Marguerite felt strongly that they should know who the father was, for future health and psychological reasons. We learned that some lesbian mothers use the sperm from several men so as *not* to know the father's identity.

The idea of bringing a child into the world as part of a lifestyle experiment still leaves us cold. As our adopted son put it, "Why didn't they settle for a kitten or a puppy?" On the other hand, we love being Teresa's grandparents regardless of her troubling origins.

When we responded so negatively to the prospect of the baby, Louisa became very upset and said we had never loved her or her friends. I confessed to having mixed feelings about some of her friends, but I certainly did love her, and I don't think she doubts that any more. I hope not. Her parenthood seemed to defuse a lot of the static electricity that had been in the air, and we all seem to be much more at ease in each other's company. We have always done our best to be welcoming to her friends, even when she seemed to be testing our response. Once, she brought an overall-clad woman to Thanksgiving dinner, a forceful person who tried to organize the occasion and who gave unsolicited but very firm advice to all the assembled relatives, and who also left her dirty sheets in a heap on the floor when she departed. For the most part, we have come to like Louisa's friends and lovers very much; I think we have all learned to trust each other.

I can't understand families who close their doors to their children for any reason. We feel very lucky to have our granddaughter, and also very fortunate to have close contact with an interesting group of people we might never have known were it not for Louisa's sexual choice.

We still worry, of course. There had been a lot of chill in our families with regard to our adopted children, and we know that any problems any of our kids have are blamed on adoption. Teresa is bound to have problems, everyone does, and they will be blamed on her parents. It is inevitable that she will have to deal with a lot of pain caused by her "difference" from the "norm." But she has excellent parents, and we're sure she'll make it. We hope they will teach her not only to be strong and confident, but also to accept the whole world without anxiety or anger.

As I look back on what I've written, I'm afraid that my stress on "acceptance" sounds condescending, too much like "tolerance." I guess there are no uncomplicated human relationships. I hope I haven't suggested that I have reached my present position unscathed, without guilt, without a heart full of painful yearning for absolution, for acceptance from my daughters. It's all very well to say that *I* accept *them*; the most obvious lesson I've learned is that I need *them* to accept *me*. I've tried to be as honest as I can about the ups and downs of being a mother of lesbians, but I hope that I have, in the process, conveyed clearly my delight in motherhood and grandmotherhood even as I have let it all hang out.

# A Very Public Statement

*I am sixty years old, black, and I'm a very large woman. I have four children. I reared them basically alone. I was divorced and after spending fruitless time trying to get the child support I was awarded, I finally gave up and did it all alone. I worked at many jobs while my children were growing up. I worked as a cook in a boarding house, a short order cook, hand finisher for a designer dress maker and a domestic worker. I only took jobs as cook and upstairs maid so that I would not have to do evening work that brought me in contact with my male employers. I worked as a ticket seller in a theatre. I worked on a ship in dry dock scaling and painting, as a nurse aid and nurse sitter. I worked as a nurse-secretary-companion, ward clerk, para-professional socialworker, and research assistant. I sold industrial insurance, electrical appliances. I worked as a surveyor f or a psychological testing service. I was a bootleg hairdresser, a paid soloist and concert singer. I baked pies and made sandwiches from my home to sell. I was a seamstress, and when I absolutely had to, I worked a full-time job just dealing with Welfare so that I could feed and house my family. That family also included my mother who was mentally ill all of my life.*

*I am currently disabled and cannot work. In part, this is from a broken neck I received when I was involved in an automobile accident in 1949. It was while I was hospitalized that I learned I was pregnant. Fern was born in the fall of 1950 when I was still wearing a cervical brace.*

*My dream before marrying was to go to college and major in biology. My father and teachers pushed me into music and toward a singing career because I had an exceptional classical voice. I was born and reared in New Orleans, where I now live.*

I actually found out that my daughter was a lesbian on television. Fern and my granddaughter Deborah no longer lived at home with me. It seemed to me Fern had changed personalities over the previous few years. Fern just sort of withdrew from our relationship which had been unusually close. We shared most things including church, social occasions, talking about almost anything, shared financial resources and also shared child-rearing. Fern was my youngest child, my most sensitive child.

I had just gotten back from the store and I received a call from Naomi, a friend to both of us. Fern had asked Naomi to call me and tell me that there was going to be a statement of some sort on television. Naomi suggested that I leave home. I asked her what was going on, but she didn't say. She was at work. She worked for the state so there was very little privacy there. But there was a certain amount of urgency in her voice, and I knew she didn't rattle easily. I took her meaning, and I drove across Lake Pontchartrain where I visit often and where I have dear friends. My friend there was the kind you can be yourself with. She knew of my difficulties and anxieties about Fern.

I was basically informed. I knew that Fern had been fired from her job. I knew that she had moved more than once since then. I knew that she was fired because of incompetency which was not true. I knew that she didn't take it lying down, and with help from the American Civil Liberties Union, she sued the state, all the way up to the governor. So there she was on television coming out of the courtroom with her attorneys. I sat there and watched her being interviewed by reporters. She was very cool, very articulate, dressed in a business suit, carrying her briefcase. They asked her if she was a lesbian and if she thought she was fired for being a lesbian, or because she truly was incompetent. And she said it was because she was a black lesbian feminist. I can be calm about it now but at the time I was just about wiped out.

My friend calmed me down for a while, until the ten o'clock news came on. It was on all the local stations, and the larger ones, too. It was reaching into four or five states.

I felt betrayed. I felt anger. I felt embarrassment.

I am an only child reared by a very conservative set of parents, which made it difficult to accept some of the things that I knew I would have to encounter. I have never been so hurt in my life. This was something I couldn't conceive of happening. My child had chosen this way of life, and had chosen to make her lesbianism so public. It seemed that I was as much the focus of attention as Fern was. I felt like I was being treated as if I had the plague. I became self-conscious about my own sexuality. I wondered if people thought that I was a lesbian. I was made to feel utter and complete failure, that I had done something dreadfully wrong with Fern, with all my children, that I was pronounced guilty with the same breath that they pronounced Fern guilty, but I didn't know of what.

My community's judgment was harsh against homosexuals, harsher with women than with men. Men were accepted or tolerated more easily. But women were not discussed except as curiosities/abominations. On the surface, the community was polite, but we knew, we talked about them. They were separate, different, not us, and *they* were not public!

My greatest anger was that she had a child. She did not have to have a child. She had wanted to have a child very badly and was in graduate school when she became pregnant. I was angry that she wasn't married, but she was very cool about it. She had not wanted to be married. But I had such a hard experience myself and I thought about how hard it is for a black woman alone to rear children. I couldn't understand why she would choose this. At the time, I was angry about her having the child, though I don't believe she was lesbian at that time.

I was very close to her child, Deborah, and knew life would be hard for her. I still feel Deborah will face a great deal of difficulty in her life.

The court case went on, and there was continued coverage. Fern didn't call to find out what my reaction was. I went back to the housing project where I lived. The neighbors were gathered around. I could feel that I was being gossiped about. It was very uncomfortable in the neighborhood. I had been in the project for almost thirty years, but it had changed from a very lovely place to one where there was a lot of crime and such. Because we had different values than others there, we dressed differently and some of our social activities were different, it made us more of a target. Criticism came from that segment who looked and said, "They had thought they were so very much and look at what has happened." Fern was a very outgoing person, very charming and sensitive, well liked, and some people were perhaps jealous of her. She had slipped from grace and they pounced on this. Even in the church. I stayed away a long time before I decided to go back. The church is so very blue-nosed and upper crust.

Fern won the battle and not the war. She established the fact that she was fired because of her political activities as well as being a lesbian and not because of incompetency. She didn't get the money she was suing for, but she did win.

We were estranged after that. She moved from place to place, possibly because of the publicity. Sometimes I thought the publicity had died down. One day, I was visiting some of my extended family. I was sitting at the counter at the kitchen, and I flipped the page and saw another article and picture of her in the paper. I remember being very angry, wondering when it would ever stop.

Since I am an only child, I felt both relieved and isolated, without support. My family asked questions and insinuated answers. Do you think she was born that way? What do lesbians do? Are there other lesbians on Fern's side of the family? Why did she make a public statement? That was what was so damning, making such a public statement!

Family, church members and others discussed Fern and me. My friends would filter out the hard stuff and let me know what people were saying. It all hurt so much. I did have friends who were supportive and understanding without being judgmental and prying. That was July, 1980.

In November, Fern went on tour with a white lesbian. She spoke and read from her writing, and the other woman performed monologues. It was to raise money for her case, or so I assume because we really didn't talk about it. On tour, she went out to San Francisco for a conference for black lesbians, and she sent me material about the conference. She called right before Thanksgiving and asked if I would mind if she brought a new friend home. Well, my older daughter and son were coming. My daughter is strict Seventh Day Adventist and very much religious. It was like a family reunion, with all the extended family. There was a great deal of anxiety, and everyone knew that this woman must be someone she was dating.

Well, her friend was much older than Fern, very poised, very stern, very well-educated. She had a harsh, abrasive personality, at least to me. I didn't care for her, and I am a woman who makes friends easily. I wondered whether it was because she was in a lesbian relationship with Fern, or whether it was because I really didn't like her. It was miserable. My oldest son was so upset that he left immediately after dinner. It was not a festive occasion.

During her "friend's" visit, Fern told me she was planning to move. I had mixed feelings because I knew I would miss her and miss my granddaughter, Deborah, but I was used to her being distant from me as I didn't visit her house much, except to drop off something or pick up Deborah. She then told me she was going to move into her friend's house, and I asked if they were "an item." Her friend replied, "Definitely, we're an item." I was worried about Deborah, who was in first grade, because I didn't think this woman would be happy with a child. Fern said she wanted to go, that it was the relationship she wanted. I wanted to turn the table over, but of course I didn't. There wasn't anything I could do about it.

She moved to California and this relationship went on. I visited the next year at Thanksgiving and stayed through Christmas. I was miserable. I had brought projects to work on and classical music for refuge, but it was hard for me to be around her partner. Apparently I was very nice to her, very hypocritical really, because Fern recently told me that the woman never knew I didn't like her. But I thought she was very bad with Deborah. Some of Fern's other friends were very kind to me, and most were lesbians. I tried to find out from them if my impressions of Fern's mate were wrong, but they also thought she didn't like Deborah. I finally told this to Fern. She understood, knew the situation wasn't good, had made a decision to leave. I visited again, but I don't think they were dating at that point, and Fern had moved away from her.

I had some counseling and tried to deal with my feelings. Because of my dislike for that woman, I had to search myself very carefully to find out why. I don't think it was because of her relationship with Fern.

Fern is now living back in New Orleans and is well-established in a relationship with a friend from graduate school, Julia, who is white. It was a surprise to me that they got involved. When she wrote me to say she was moving back, she said she hoped there was nothing else she would do to cause me any heartache or embarrassment.

Most of the women in their group are from out-of-town and I felt angry that I was the only mother who lived close by and had to bear the brunt of the changes in her daughter. I expressed this and pointed out that most of them were from away, some from very wealthy families, most of them white. I know that the white community can be very judgmental about these things, but the black community can be very cruel, particularly within the group of people that I basically deal with. I had a great deal of anger about it. I told Fern once that if she had to be lesbian and live that kind of lifestyle, I had hoped she would not come back home.

Part of her being lesbian is a political statement. She is a crusader. And in doing social work, she has seen a lot of women suffer. In my own relationships with men, I was very clear about not taking abuse, and I had searched myself to see if there weren't things I had said to her to cause her to be a lesbian. After a lot of searching and some counseling, I don't believe I had anything to do with it. She is an adult with her own choices.

I still very much do not like her being a lesbian, mostly because of Deborah. I keep saying that, but I have to be honest, I don't like it! But I have accepted it.

Fern's mate, Julia, is a very warm person, very kind to me, and has helped me in many, many ways. She is also a crusader, a crusader for civil rights. I accept her. Julia is very dedicated to Deborah and tries to do everything she can to enrich her life and make it interesting. She couldn't be nicer to Deborah than if she had given birth to her. Deborah knows her mother is a lesbian, they have discussed it, and she finds it difficult because of her friends. I think this will get more difficult for her as she gets older.

I live in a retirement center. Most people are older than I and there are mixed ethnic backgrounds. It's run by nuns— one of the most difficult orders—who haven't stepped far into the twentieth century. I needed to be in a safe community, but had some ambivalence about moving here. I was very uptight about Fern and her friends visiting here, she and her mate coming together. This has been discussed, but no one has approached me. Many times Julia comes to pick up Deborah, or do things for me. She has taken a lot of flack from the black people here. It's not just black people who experience racism.

The interracial part is difficult for Deborah. Once, when she was getting picked up from day camp by Julia, the kids asked her who the white woman was. She's very bright and sharp and she said, "Oh, that's the maid!" I think Julia was hurt, not because she said she was the maid but because she wants to be considered a parent. But Deborah said to me the other day, "I am very fortunate, I have two mommies and three grandmothers." She included Julia's mother.

Last year, Fern invited me to a black women's retreat. In her sharing, she made a declaration of love. It was quite an emotional experience. She stated that we had been estranged for about six years and said that she had grown to realize how much she loved me and how much she had angered and hurt me. In a group of about fifty women, she asked for forgiveness and asked that we be closer. Many things are getting better.

PAULINE JOHNSON

# Ways of Knowing and Not Knowing

*I'm an English teacher in a small city in Northern California. I have two heterosexual daughters, one lesbian daughter, and three grandchildren. I grew up in the Midwest and moved to California after I married. I am separated from my husband who has never been told that Paula is a lesbian. Paula and her partner of four years, Donna, live in a small community near the California coast.*

I'm not sure how far back to go, so I will start with Paula's childhood. She was one of those bright, organized children who does well in school and has one or two close friends at a time. She has a high I.Q., and there were few tasks that she wouldn't take on. Things she couldn't do she taught herself, like riding a bike or jumping rope.

She dated very little in high school, but in college had a couple of good men friends of long standing. In her last year of college, she and Meg became roommates and lovers, though I didn't know the latter for a couple of years.

I have several gay friends and have been an accepting friend and supportive person to them. When Paula came out to me she said, "I know how accepting you have been of your gay friends. I hope you'll be as accepting of me." She thought at that time that she was bisexual because she had been in some intimate relationships with men.

I guess I had suspected it all for some time. My initial feeling was that she would never experience the joy of having children. When I examined that feeling, I realized it was a selfish one in that I wanted her to have grandchildren for *me*. With two other daughters, one now married and the mother of three sons, I am not bereft of grandchildren.

I told Paula that who she told was up to her. She gave me permission to tell my closest friends. I told her that she should tell her father herself. *She never has. He never mentions it.* She brought Meg, and now her partner Donna, home with her frequently and to our family get-togethers. She called me once to say that she and Alan, a young man with whom she works, would meet me at the movies. Her father asked me if she was dating him. I told him I didn't think so. Since she has never told him outright, I cannot discuss it with him. He avoids words like *homosexual, gay* and *lesbian.* I asked her what would happen if he found out now. She said that she would tell him that if she was heterosexual, she wouldn't discuss her sex life with him, and that's why she has never felt like she had to tell him of her lesbianism.

As for me, I have found having a lesbian daughter an enriching experience; as her "accepting" parent, I am included in feminist concerts she and her friends attend. I sat in an ice cream parlor one night with a dozen women, and looking around discovered to my amazement that I was the only "straight" woman at the table!

I am active in the Presbyterian church, and sometimes that is difficult for me. Presbyterians as a whole are generally hardnosed about including gay and lesbian people in membership—chiefly because any members can become an officer and, as they think, God forbid we should have homosexuals making important decisions and setting a bad example for the flock!

ALICE WONG

# A Fashion Crisis

*I have worked for the United States government my whole life and am currently the National Import Specialist for Dolls and Toys. It's a great job. Since 1988, I have been involved with PFLAG, and am also active in the First Unitarian Church. I am a widow, and have one child, Ellen, who is Asian-American.*

Hindsight is so helpful. Now I know why Ellen was such a difficult child.

Rereading these opening words, I had to stop and laugh. How like a straight parent to assume that my troubles with my daughter when she was very young were because she was aware she was different and that difference was that she was a lesbian! Our difference could have been because we are both very strong willed—read *stubborn*—women.

From an early age, Ellen had strong opinions. She fought me on what she would wear, and this became a major battle area. She hated dresses, bright colors or pastels. Generally I fussed and fumed, but I did not force her to wear a dress or skirt. Ellen did things in her own good time. (She still does!) However, when she was young and I more rigid, I would get upset that she would not do her chores as soon as I asked her to. Because I was demanding and critical, she was withdrawn and sullen around me.

Although Ellen and I had not been close when she was a child, the death of her father when she was eleven forced me to grow up and become a better parent (a parent more like her dad from whom she had received wonderful support and unconditional love). Once I relaxed and learned to enjoy being a parent, I came to like my child and enjoy her company. I learned that I had a funny, deep and very mature teenage daughter. We talked about everything. In a short time, we became very close. It is sad that it took my husband's death for me to learn to be a good parent.

However, even though we had become close and were talking about everything, Ellen hesitated to tell me about being gay. She feared I would not be able to handle it and would revert back to my old critical ways. For quite a while before she told me, I suspected she was gay. Her strong opinions on how she should look were one clue. But the most convincing evidence was that she raised the subject of homosexuality in conversations with me on a fairly regular basis, something the average teenager does not do with a parent. Sometime in her fifteenth year (1984), we were again waltzing around the subject of homosexuality. I asked Ellen if she were gay. As she now explains, she was so surprised to finally be confronted that she did not have the presence of mind to lie. Of course, I had to ask the universal question, "Are you sure?" Ellen told me she knew from a very young age that she was different.

Since I already suspected, I really wasn't surprised. To be honest, it was a relief to have it out in the open. I do not remember being upset. I remember saying we would have to do some reading to "find out what we have to do." In reality, I sent Ellen down to Greenwich Village to find some books.

Being the strong-willed person she is, Ellen decided that if she were a lesbian, she would act like one. She was young and she did not have much access to information, so she followed the stereotypes and conformed to what other lesbians were doing. At that time, this meant dressing in black, wearing pants and men's clothes. She always wore big chunky boots and this was long before they were fashionable. She would never wear dresses and had no interest in make-up or other things traditionally associated with girls. She was interested in sports and generally would not (and still does not) show too much emotion.

Even before I knew she was gay, I had stopped putting up much of a fight on the dark clothes and lack of dresses, but I drew the line on wearing black as I did not believe young girls should. I believe that particular dictate was handed down to me by my mother. We have a funny story about it. One day when Ellen and I were on the way to a movie, she spotted a skirt and blouse in a store window which she immediately liked. Since it was a skirt, I marched right into the store and had her try it on, bought it without asking the price, and made no comment about the fact that it was black silk, except to say black looked good on her. She was a junior in high school. Although at this time in her life, I knew she was gay, I was so happy she was interested in a skirt, I bought it for her without thought or hesitation even thought it was clearly too sophisticated an outfit for her age and even though it was black!

I put my foot down on the chunky shoes. I do not find chunky shoes attractive. I love shoes but, because of my big feet, I have a limited range to choose from. I could not understand anyone purposely wanting ugly shoes. Of course, if I am honest with myself, in the back of my mind was the thought that even though Ellen was a lesbian, I did not want her to look like one.

I come from a very liberal background and I have lived in New York City most of my life. My parents taught tolerance and acceptance from as early as I can remember. My liberal religion, Unitarianism, not only does not condemn homosexuality, it acknowledges it as a normal aspect of human sexuality. So once I got over the fashion crisis, it was not difficult for me to accept the fact that Ellen was gay.

After she was out to me, Ellen began to tell her very good friends in high school and I encouraged her to do so. I remember telling her she had an obligation to do so because if it came out that she was gay, her friends would be "tarnished with the same brush" and therefore, they had a right to know. As far as I know, no one she was close to turned away from her. She informed me she was going to be completely out in college, a concept I was in agreement with.

Living a lie is too much work and not healthy. Of course, all my words of wisdom to my daughter were not necessarily applied to me. I told only a very few good friends about her. My closest friends would have to know, so that if I were upset about something that had to do with Ellen, I could talk to them about it. Generally though, I was not out that I had a lesbian daughter.

This "do as I say, not as I do" behavior came home to me in 1987 when I read about the Gay Rights March in Washington, D.C. An article in the *New York Times* by a very proud parent spoke of his warm supportive feelings for his daughter. I was convinced that Ellen had been at the parade and I was upset that, although I had those same strong feelings about my daughter, I had not been at that parade. Even worse, I had not even known about the parade.

I called Ellen, who was away at college, and asked if she had attended the parade. Of course she had. I asked her what I should be doing to support her. The article made me realize I needed to be as "out" as my daughter. Ellen gave me the name PFLAG, Parents and Friends of Lesbians and Gays.

At first, I was disappointed with PFLAG. The meetings are mainly for people who are having trouble accepting the information about their children. Many of the parents coming to PFLAG meetings are very upset that their child is gay. They feel guilty, thinking they have done something to cause their child's condition. They feel they have been cheated out of certain rights and privileges of being a parent. Although I had not been overly public about having a gay child, I had never viewed it as a tragedy. I found some of the hysterics a little hard to take. I feel that parents should be honored and proud that their children love and trust them enough to tell them the truth. My whole purpose for attending the PFLAG meetings was to be completely out and supportive of my daughter and the gay community. Of course, once I got involved with the organization and moved beyond the meetings, I was more busy.

I started coming out about Ellen to everyone. The way I would usually raise the subject is to say that I could not do something on a certain weekend because I was going to a PFLAG meeting. I would then explain what PFLAG stood for and reveal that Ellen was gay. Generally, since I was so casual about it, I got a casual response. One time, however, I remember becoming annoyed when a friend began to commiserate with me after I told her. I felt angry that she offered her sympathy.

The way Ellen and I "came out" to our church was to announce that we were going to be on a *Geraldo!* show about lesbians and their mothers. This was after the 1989 Washington, D.C. march when I realized my need to be more involved in "the movement." I received a number of favorable comments the next Sunday from people who had watched the show.

To be honest, during the first years, if I were having a bad day and feeling sorry for myself, or upset about life in general, I would add Ellen being gay to the list of my woes. I know I was saddened to think her career choices would be limited. And in the beginning, I did not see any need for her to "advertise" she was gay.

But that has changed. Now I would not want her any other way than how she is. She dresses in dark colors, mostly black, and she looks great. The shoes are mostly boots, but not all that chunky. The hair is short and when she is dressed up in her suits—men's—she is frequently addressed as "sir." She is the unique person she is, in part, because she is gay. I have qualms about her motorcycle, but those fears are about the safety of motorcycles, and have nothing to do with her being a lesbian. Selfishly, I must add that my life is different because Ellen is a lesbian. I think I am a better person for having to deal with the issue. I know the closeness Ellen and I have is due, in part, to the fact that after being able to tell me she was a lesbian, there was no other subject we could not talk about. Just because we talk and share our feelings and attitudes, however, does not mean I agree with everything Ellen says or does. I still reserve my right as a parent to point out the error of her ways.

I am very close to my daughter, closer than I may have a right to be. Moreover, I have been exposed to a whole different world. I follow the happenings in the gay community and consider myself an honorary member. I have been forced to grow as a person and I certainly have a purpose in life. I have met many of Ellen's wonderful friends and have had the sad honor of being the parent they could talk to instead of their own. I always feel sad for their parents who are missing out on the wonderful intimacy they might have had with their children. Most of all, it is truly remarkable how proud a gay child is about having an openly supportive parent.

RAQUEL J.

# Another Kind of Different

*I am retired now. I had four children and one of my sons passed away a few years ago. I divorced my husband when my daughter Chrissy was about ten, so it was basically she and I. I am Mexican-American, born and raised in San Francisco.*

From the time Christine was a young girl, a child really, I knew she was different. Every mother thinks her child is different in a special way, but this was another kind of difference. Since I had a gay sister who had a very difficult time because of her generation and my mother, I decided I just wasn't going to make the same mistake with Chrissy. My mother was from Mexico, very old-fashioned with old-country thinking. I have been fortunate to be exposed to a lot more than she was. She knew what my sister was, but she couldn't cope with homosexuality at all. She had no one to talk to and, of course, my sister did not talk to her either. It was very difficult and I learned a lot of lessons from growing up in that environment.

During those few years when Chrissy was growing up, the adolescent years and early teenage years, life was very difficult for her. It was because of her sexuality, I'm sure of it. I don't think she knew it, or if she did, she didn't understand. I suspected very strongly that she was gay. She wasn't interested in dating, and she attached herself to girlfriends, as do most girls, but this was different. It's so hard to explain; it was just little things that I saw.

When Chrissy was in her early teens, she felt like she had to get away from me to discover her identity. I crossed my fingers and let her go. I knew she was too young, but she was going to go anyway. It broke my heart because I was so worried about her. She went to Oregon and I think it was then that she met a lot of gay women who took her in under their wing.

I started getting letters from her, and I got the picture that she was with a lot of people who she could really relate to. Maybe they were surrogate mothers; they all sort of took care of her. She was learning about herself and maybe learning how she could tell me about herself. I already knew this! But couldn't tell her; I felt she should tell me. She came back a year later, at sixteen, much matured, and she told me she was a lesbian. Of course, I wasn't surprised and I told her so. I have always accepted her.

The women whom my sister knew were very unhappy people. I suppose they were going through what my sister was going through, with her mother and with society's view of homosexuals at that time. There was a lot of turmoil, a lot of drinking, and they were very different from the lesbians I have come to know through Chrissy. Her friends are wonderful people and I love them. Chrissy brings her friends home to visit and it's wonderful. I'm on my third husband now, I'm settled, I enjoy life and really enjoy Chrissy.

My husband, David, has never been exposed to the gay world. He's very giving, shy, and somewhat old-fashioned, but if people are happy he thinks that's fine. The ironic part of it all is that his son is gay, too. I talk to his son about it, but it's hard for him to talk to his father. His mother, my husband's first wife, died several years ago and was a totally different person than his father. I guess she never would have understood homosexuality. Maybe God took care of that for him, I don't know. My husband accepts Chrissy, and she and her friends are welcome in our house. What they do behind the bedroom door is their business. Life for all of us would be very different if I was still married to Chrissy's father. I don't think he would have understood.

I feel that gay women have a more difficult time in life than other women. People are coming around, but not as fast as I'd like to see it. People express so many social attitudes that will always keep a gay person down, with jobs, and with children. Chrissy now wants very much to have a child. I can understand it. Most women—gay or not—want children in their lives. I have never been crazy about other people's babies, so I'd just as soon she carries the child. I'm afraid of hurting Chrissy if her partner has a child and I can't feel as though that child is part of me. I want to feel that bond, so I want her to carry the child. At the same time, I don't want her to go through all the difficulty of pregnancy.

It's going to be difficult for her. She is in school now and I would prefer that she waits until she finishes to have a child. Raising children takes a lot of time. It's hard; I did it. But that's another part of the lesbian life she is leading. If you are a twenty-six-year old heterosexual woman and you've gone to college, you marry a man with a good job, buy a house and settle down and raise children. But for lesbians, it's not like that, they have to do it all themselves and it's difficult, even with a partner.

DARLENE PALMER

# A Second Chance

Lori was the child I never thought I'd have. I had been told I might never get pregnant, and so when I found I was, I felt God had blessed me. Eleven months later, our son Mike was born and fourteen months later, a second daughter, Teri.

As the years went by and all the other little girls were having crushes on the little boys, I kept waiting for Lori to find a special friend, but she never seemed interested. For several years, she was very interested in being with Carol, the daughter of one of my close friends.

*I am the mother of three children, two girls and a boy each a year apart in birth. I love being a wife, mother and home-maker. I grew up in the Congrega-tional Church, studied and was a deaconess in the Presbyterian Church, and now am a member of the United Church of Christ. Since the children got out of high school, I have been an avid tennis player.*

When Lori was in the eighth grade, we moved several hundred miles away. At that time, I began to wonder why Lori was still not interested in boys, and homosexuality came to mind. I put that out of my head by telling myself that she just wasn't ready for boys yet. In high school, she went to all the games and dances, and was involved in band and athlet-ics. She was well-known for her athletic ability. Eventually, she became very close to one special girl, and I became con-cerned about the way she had begun to act at home—very hostile, unhappy and removed. It was a gradual change in her behavior and I thought it was part of the teenage years.

One evening I was reading in the living room and over-heard her talking on the phone with her girlfriend. She was unaware I was there, and she talked about something that had happened at the principal's office. It sounded as if she had gotten away with whatever it was. Later, I told her I was in the room and asked her about what happened. She told me a reasonable story, that a mistake had been made by the school. Later, I felt uncomfortable with what she had said. I debated going to the school because I knew she would think I didn't trust her. It was a terrible decision to make, but eventually, I went to talk with a counselor about her behavior and unhappiness.

I found she had more than twenty absences, and the principal and I called Lori in to talk. She would say nothing. I knew she could be tough. After what seemed like hours, I got onto her and finally broke her down. She said, "Mom, I need help. I think I am a lesbian."

It didn't shock me, but I hated hearing it. I felt as though my secret thoughts about her were now part of our lives. She had been cutting classes to pick up her girlfriend, Pam, the girl she had been obsessed with for several months.

Lori went back to class and I talked with the principal about where I could get help. She told me to see our family doctor, and he gave me the name of a psychiatrist. Her father came back after being out of town for a few days, and though he didn't have much reaction to the news that I could see, he said we would give her all the help she needed and was supportive of me.

At the first meeting, the psychiatrist asked me how I thought Lori had become "this way." I thought about Lori's life and all that I had observed and I said that I thought she was born this way. He said, "No. You and your husband have done something in the family home that made her this way." I was crushed. Then he said that because Lori had not had a sexual lesbian encounter, he thought he could change her. I believed him and was relieved that Lori would eventually be all right.

Things seemed to get worse. Lori hated Dr. Brown, and begged not to go to him, but he had said she would do that. I started finding poems in her room, love poems addressed to Pam. I also found many poems about death and dying and told the doctor about them. He said he didn't think

Lori would do anything to herself, but I worried about her killing herself.

Once, in a particularly bad scene, she wouldn't tell us what was going on. She kept saying, "I can't tell you, it's too terrible." I had a strange gutsy feeling and I said, "Lori, are you afraid you are going to hurt yourself?" She said yes, and told us she had tried several times while doing the dishes to shove a butcher knife into herself.

Again, my deepest fears had been realized. I knew how desperate she was, and tried to be home when she was so nothing could happen. For two years things didn't get better. Her attitude was very bad, and she even ran away once. Another time, I threw her out of the house because of her actions towards us. I prayed to God to take back this child. Since I could do nothing for her maybe it was up to him to guide her back to normal.

When Lori was about to graduate from high school, we stopped seeing Dr. Brown and began to see a minister from an Episcopal Church. Lori liked him. He said he wasn't going to change her, but try to help her accept herself as whatever she turned out to be. At this time, she made plans to go into the military service. She left for boot camp a few weeks after graduation.

Lori spent the next eight years in Germany. They were years that I felt free of the burden, the guilt, the shame, the hatred of having a lesbian daughter. When she came home twice for short periods of time, we could not communicate. I hated her being home, and looked forward to her being gone so I'd be free again. I couldn't feel any love for her, not when I felt she was hurting me so.

During those eight years, Lori sent letters of awards and commendations. She was commended for her performance, her enthusiasm, knowledge, and technical expertise. One said she "exemplified the motto 'Pride in Service.'" Another stated her "individual performance was an example others should follow."

There were also pictures with some of the awards and commendations, one of which I am particularly proud. Lori had been selected as an outstanding military person and one part of the honor was acting as commander for the day which included an inspection of the troops. With silver helmet on her head, the American flag in the background, and surrounded by her personal assistants, she is shown receiving the lined-up troops as they are saluting her.

But when she would anticipate a trip home, I would feel uptight and scared. I told my minister of my feelings, of wanting Lori to come home, but being afraid of her coming home. He was able to help me understand some of my feelings. I began to understand why I felt as I did, and that it wasn't unusual for some parents to react as I did. I felt I had learned something about myself, but had still not accepted Lori or her homosexuality.

Her sister was going to get married, and neither of her siblings knew she was a lesbian. I encouraged Lori to come home to be in the wedding. She came home for six weeks, and things went from bad to worse during that time. This resulted in her not wanting to be part of the wedding. It even got to the point where she left the house for three or four days and we didn't know where she was. My friends noticed that something was wrong and tried to get me to talk about it. They even asked if my marriage was all right. I told them it had to do with the children, which they could understand, but of course, I couldn't let anyone know my problem was that my daughter was a lesbian.

One of my friends suggested that I find a support group for whatever it was that was bothering me, and I spent two days calling churches and referral services before I finally found someone who could give me the name of another mother who had a gay child. I contacted this woman who was part of Parents and Friends of Lesbians and Gays and we talked about my feelings and about things she had felt. The key that opened a special door for me was when she told me to allow myself to accept the love Lori was giving me, and then to try to return that love. She said if I did, I would find a very special love with my gay child, unlike the love between myself and my other children.

These were the most positive words I had heard for as long as I had known about homosexuality, and the most important ones.

I started to talk to Lori, though we only had three or four days of her six-week stay to learn about each other in what was to be a new relationship between a mother and her child.

After Lori went back to the military, I started to attend a Parents and Friends of Lesbians and Gays support group and read books on homosexuality. I found myself in an area of life of which I was totally ignorant, but found acceptance in the group and no longer felt alone. I look back at what happened between my child and me, and I know that in those last few days before Lori had to leave home, it was as if I literally held her life in my hands. I could destroy her or accept her love. Maybe it was necessary for me to have suffered such pain, guilt, shame and heartache in order that I might be where I am today. I now understand more of what children go through when they realize they are homosexual and how they must learn to accept themselves.

I felt my hate turn to love; my shame turn to pride, my pain to joy, and my guilt to freedom. Today, Lori and I are not only mother and daughter, we are best of friends. I have been given a second chance on a child I almost lost. For this, I thank God—and PFLAG.

My fear today is about the military and Lori's homosexuality. They state that being homosexual is a security risk. It is believed that homosexuals could be blackmailed into giving military secrets because they are not out of the closet, either to their parents or the military. If the military found out about her lesbianism, Lori could be dishonorably discharged with the possibility of prison. My heart still feels an ache for this injustice which Lori must live with each day. She has given nine years of service and is planning on a military career—if they will allow her to serve. And they will, as long as they see her as someone she is not.

The road for parent, or for child, can be filled with hate, guilt, shame and alienation. But that is not the only path. There is also a road toward a special love, a freedom, a pride and an acceptance.

# Towards a Bright Future

*I have recently moved to a new state and am busy unpacking. Normally I work as a physical rehabilitation nurse. I am also a member of Alcoholics Anonymous, and have been for many, many years. I was a housewife and "stay at home" mother for twenty-one years.*

Holly is now twenty-five. She is the third of three children. A cute kid, she grew up in a normal fashion. She was always a tomboy, especially compared to her sister who is three years older, feminine and outgoing. Holly has quite a different personality. She is quiet and clingy, especially to her father. In high school, she didn't do anything special to look pretty. This baffled me then and still does. Holly just doesn't make an effort to look her absolute best. To me, she is an attractive person, with small and delicate features, although she envies the feminine slimness of her sister and myself.

Although she grew up in several countries, she seemed like a normal kid. She was athletic and participated in soccer, swimming and other sports. A good part of her growing up took place in Italy and Belgium. I'm sure there was the turmoil of adjustment to living here and there. For all my kids, making and losing friends was a part of life. Holly seemed to fare worse at this; she didn't make many long-term friendships, and was very dependent on our family for support.

When Holly was in high school, my sister was in a severe accident. I had to leave the family off and on for several years to help arrange her affairs and guide her in head-injury rehab. Holly stayed with her father in Belgium and she really bonded with him. Back in the States for her last year of high school, Holly had sporadic boyfriends. They would show up for several weeks and then disappear. In retrospect, I think this was a time of experimenting with sex, and alcohol.

In college, Holly joined a sorority. I don't think she dated much, though the last year she had a boyfriend. He visited us a few times and we still see him occasionally. He's a little kooky but we learned to like him very much. He moved when Holly went on to graduate school and it seemed like she didn't date anyone. I wondered why. I thought, "Isn't that too bad." She did well in school, but didn't have a whole lot else going on.

Holly had been very depressed, and in the last year of school, she had gone on anti-depressants. It had been a battle finding a medication that worked for her. Her father is a psychiatrist and I am a nurse so both of us tried to find something to help her. We were very worried about her because there is a family history of depression. Both of us believe that depression is inherited, a biochemical process, and that as a disease, it should not hold the stigma that it does in society.

Six months ago, Holly said she had something to tell us. She thought she was a lesbian. She had come up with the idea, and she couldn't tell us exactly why. There were a lot of tears. "I finally understand myself," she said. "I have tried to be normal by dating men, but I enjoy being with women a lot more than men."

At that point, Holly said she had had no intimate contact with another woman. I felt like I had swallowed a bag of cement. In the following couple of weeks, I asked some questions and tried to get a few things clarified. Each bit of information helped decrease the feeling in my stomach. Suddenly a couple of women showed up from a neighboring town. One of them already had a partner, so I figured she was Holly's buddy, but I could tell Holly really liked the other one. Both women are very nice, and I am happy Holly had made such nice friends.

After Holly came out, I spent a lot of time crying. I just couldn't believe it and I couldn't talk about it much. Intermittently, I have shared my feelings with my small AA group.

My group had been supportive but I know there are people there that do not accept gays and lesbians as healthy people. In my heart, I wondered if not being out was partly a cause of Holly's depression, and I hoped she could finally be happy.

I still have so much sadness, even though I know it is selfish. I wanted to have grandchildren from her. My other daughter is now married so I am sad there will be no more weddings. I was also worried about her siblings' reactions, though both my son and daughter seem to be quite okay with it. But, except for Holly, my family doesn't talk much about emotional issues. Holly is a good listener and I'm sure she would talk a bundle if I knew what to ask her. But I don't know what to talk to her about.

At this point, the initial shock and loss has settled somewhat, but I just want to see her thrive. Holly is the one I worry about the most, and maybe I shouldn't. She is an intelligent, creative, dependable and caring person. Perhaps she'll be fine and one of the other children will end up with problems.

My husband and I have had lots of contact with the gay community through AIDS work, he as a lecturer and I as a nurse. We attended numerous gay functions and felt comfortable and accepting of this population before Holly came out to us. I think our experiences helped decrease the shock of her announcement.

But my husband and I rarely talk about it. Initially he was eager to receive information about her life. Basically, he said it was certainly okay but thought it would be hard for her. Lesbians have to struggle more in life, there are more ups and downs. There is social discrimination and I think it is difficult to maintain close marital-type relationships. When Holly applied for the Peace Corps, she made the mistake of being honest about her history of depression and she was disqualified. Now I have told her not to mention the depression or anything about being a lesbian, unless she is in a situation where she would benefit from being out.

I have told my one best friends. Her comment was, "Wasn't it nice that she told you?" I won't tell anyone without consulting Holly first. It's like with alcoholism; you don't tell everybody or expect everyone to understand and accept you.

An old, dear friend of mine who lives nearby is lesbian. She has lived with the same lover for many years. I respect and adore them both. This makes me feel optimistic about Holly's chances for a positive relationship. I pray every day that her future will be bright, both socially and careerwise. Each day I feel more at ease with my daughter's choice.

DOROTHY A. TOLLIFSON

# "Winnetka Matron Testifies for Gay Rights"

*I was born in Wisconsin in 1909, and have lived most of my life in Chicago. I have worked as a typist, stenographer, and an editor, and was even fired from the A&P while working there to make money for college—I never could manage to get the tub butter out of the tub and into one of those cardboard boxes! I married late to just about the dearest man in the world. He died a few years ago and I moved into the city from the suburbs—I love city life. Here, it's possible to get about easily at night and I go to as many theater, opera and music programs as I can.*

In the first place, our daughter was born without a right hand. Now, that was a considerable shock to both my husband and me, and something which we knew we must deal with. We were concerned about seeing to it that this youngster would be able to do whatever she might want to do. Our concerns for her early years were to make it possible for her to learn to do all the things the other youngsters did.

As a young child, my daughter had many more young boys as playmates than girls, principally because that's who was around in the neighborhood. As the years went on, she had loads of girl friends but was not an outstanding success with the boys. I did not think this especially strange because when I was in high school, many years before, I was not an outstanding success with the boys either, and so I simply assumed that she had somehow been endowed with that particular bit of me.

When she went away to college and came home with a young woman friend, we began to wonder. Also in her high school and college years, she had several friends with whom she spent a good deal of time, and we wondered about these associations. I wish I could remember when she told us, but I cannot. I think perhaps we gradually became aware of it, although perhaps she did actually tell us—if she did, I do not remember it. I do know that neither my husband nor I were shocked or dismayed by the knowledge that she was a lesbian. We knew a number of homosexuals and lesbians, and had known them for a long time. Our main concern was for her. We knew life would be more difficult for her because of this and because of the misunderstanding which exists about these people. We also knew that as far back as you can go in history, you will find homosexuals as part of society, and in most cases, seemingly accepted by it—which may or may not be true as history is always sieved through a particular person. We knew, however, of the misunderstanding about homosexuals in the community in which we lived.

I think perhaps all parents have a dream of their children growing up, marrying, having children, and living happily ever after. I was fortunate in that I had a very happy marriage. My husband is dead now, but he was a man of unusual understanding.

There is a church in Chicago where parents can go for dialogue with others and for help and support. I went to a few meetings and tried to project the fact that my husband and I were not troubled because our daughter was a lesbian. We were having trouble because society comes down so heavily on those people.

I have done volunteer work for many years for a group that works for police accountability. We work with the victims of police abuse, police harassment or excessive use of force. In this work, we are aware of how law enforcement people treat the members of the gay community. Because of this knowledge, we naturally were concerned that perhaps our daughter would encounter abuse at some point from law enforcement personnel.

The Illinois legislature was considering a bill to open housing and employment and all other civil rights to homosexuals and lesbians, and I went to Springfield to testify in favor of the bill. I must say the committee before which we appeared was most unsympathetic about the whole problem.

As I left the chamber, I was asked by a reporter how old I was, and where I lived and other such irrelevant questions the media usually ask, and I answered him. The following morning the *Chicago Tribune* ran a three-column, four-inch story, captioned *Winnetka Matron Testifies for Gay Rights*.

About a month later, someone called me from Waukegan, a city in northern Illinois, and asked if I would appear there in favor of gay rights. I went there and testified. I said that I wanted my daughter to have the same rights as other people in society, that everyone should have the same rights. As I left, a woman came to talk to me. Her daughter had told her she was a lesbian and she didn't know what to do about it. I tried to tell her to love her daughter and to accept her the way she is. She telephoned me several times after that and we talked. That seemed to help her.

A good friend, who also lived in Winnetka, called me one day. She asked me about a story which had appeared in the *Tribune* some months before, and I finally realized she was asking me about testifying for the gay rights bill. She told me that she had just discovered that her son was gay and she did not know how to handle it—she was devastated. It so happened that I was going to a fundraising event for some gay issue, and I invited her to come with me. I said I would introduce her to a lot of homosexual men and she would be able to see that they are really very nice and don't grow horns or anything else odd! Well, she came, and I asked several of my friends at the event to talk with her, especially about accepting the fact that her son had told her he was gay. She came away with a much broader understanding of the whole issue. Happily, she and her son are wonderful friends now, and she knows and accepts him.

I have met my daughter's friends over the years and I have formed some very lasting friendships with some of her friends. They are all wonderful and I am very proud of her and of what she does and of the kind of a woman she is. Because the kind of a woman she is, is wonderful.

JEAN CAMERON

*I'm sixty-two and retired from working twenty-eight years as a librarian.*

# Like Daughter, Like Mother

Erna used to write boys' names on her school books so I naturally thought she was in every way "normal." She excelled in school, but when I moved her and her younger brother to a new town, she was sent home to lengthen the same skirt that was acceptable at her old school. This marked the beginning of the rebellion. She wasn't challenged at school, and started to experiment with drugs. Wrongly, I assumed the entire problem was hers and I tried to get therapy for her. Our relationship reached an impasse and I had no power over her. I came home from work one day when she was thirteen to find a note telling me that she had run away. In the note, she told me not to worry.

I finally found her at a home for runaways. I gave my permission for her to be able stay there for two weeks. But after the two weeks, she didn't come home. She ran away again. And she traveled. She called me from time to time, from hog farms and communes, and she always let me know she was okay. During this time, I was quite detached from my feelings. I just felt like there was nothing I could do to change her or get her back.

Several years later, I remarried and Erna came home for the wedding. After the ceremony, she stayed on with her paternal grandparents, took the high school equivalency exam, and enrolled in community college even though she was only fifteen.

Two years later, she entered a university where she was very happy. Then one day, she called to tell me she was bringing home a woman friend. Imagining an older person, I was amazed to see that her friend was a contemporary.

This is when she told me she was gay. "That's nice, Erna, I'm glad you're happy" was my polite reply.

My memory of the next few days is very vague. But I soon began to read about lesbianism, listen to gay radio programs and I even attended a meeting of the Daughters of Bilitis, a lesbian social group with branches all over the country. One day I left a note on the ladies' room door at work, "Are there any DOB's here?" Later I saw someone had penciled in the word *yes.*

Now what?! Soon thereafter, a call came to me from the office of the Fortune 500 company at which I worked as a librarian. "What's DOB?" I was asked. Terrified, I reached for a copy of the *Encyclopedia of Acronyms* and started reading the very long list of DOBs. With my heart in my mouth, I finally came to *the* one. "A woman's organization," I read to my inquirer. The next time I went to the ladies' room, my sign was down. I never tried that again.

Talking about Erna's orientation embarrassed me. Also, she felt I was a lesbian and told me so. I didn't believe she could be right. I asked her about older gay women, but all she told me was that gay women get older, too. I asked her how she could "tell" if a woman was gay. "You can just tell," she said. A fat lot of good that did me! I was terrified of finding out about myself so we avoided the subject altogether.

Erna and I had never had a really close relationship, and from the time she came out to me, she always brought another woman home with her. I was uncomfortable with her bringing her partners home because I always had some man in the wings who might "catch on" to her being gay. I loved Erna, but was terrified that someone might find out about her. In fact, I walked with the same woman every noontime for ten years and I never told her about Erna. The silence lasted a long time.

Then, several years ago right before my retirement, I wondered what I might do with my life. I was on my own and absently picked up a book about options for retirement.

It spoke of RVs (recreational vehicles), vans with their own baths, kitchens and beds. Aha! Travelling! It sounded just like what I wanted to do. I began to read all about this lifestyle. In a magazine about trailer life, I spotted an ad for a women's RV club. I signed up immediately. I needed an RV of my own, and so I bought one sight unseen from an RV mag. I flew to another state, was instructed in some of the ins and outs of the "rig" and drove home. By the time I had cleared city limits, I knew I would love both the rig and the life.

In the fall of that year, I attended my first RV Women rally. There were hands-on sessions on the care and feeding of our RVs, pot lucks and all kinds of social interaction. After the rally, I knew I wanted only to be in the company of women, and I began to understand Erna. When it became apparent that we hated the rally to end, it was a natural progression to form a community! After a long search, the Pueblo was founded.

The Pueblo is a women's RV park in Apache Junction, Arizona. It is the first of its kind anywhere. There are a total of four hundred fifty lots and on New Year's Eve, the busiest time in this fine winter climate, we have parties with over one thousand women. Erna supported my plan to sell the house and everything in it and move to the Pueblo. In fact, she imagined me doing this before I did!

I own a space with a friend named Erna. Many of the women here are lesbians. Many are mothers. Some are widowed, and some, like myself, divorced. Others are retired military, nurses, and lawyers. All are happy to be here making community.

I came here as a straight woman, but I was soon caught up in the closeness of the community and realized I could never live in a heterosexual world again. Here, I am loved for who I am and I can speak my truth. For the first time in my life, I feel very free. I have declared myself to be lesbian, although I have yet to have a partner in the fullest sense. I'm very comfortable with the loving relationships I see around me here at the Pueblo and I am accepted with love for who I am—a self-proclaimed lesbian, albeit single. Erna reminded me that she knew I was gay many years ago, and just waited patiently until I knew it too. It took the Pueblo for that to happen.

Since living here, I've gone through a lot of therapy dealing with all the emotions I'd never let myself feel, including my love for my daughter. I discovered that I had repeated my own experience of abandonment by my mother with my own daughter. One day in my therapy group, I announced that I was going to become a mother. I didn't know how I would do it, at sixty years old, with my daughter three thousand miles away, but I began a journey.

Erna has dealt with my seeming abandonment of her when she was a teenager. She gave me a journal and I began to write in it all my memories and experiences about her, everything I could remember from when she was born onwards. It was a very cathartic experience. I left out nothing, including my guilt and my alcoholism. To her surprise, I sent the journal to her.

It's been twenty-three years since Erna came out to me. But today, we're our authentic selves with one another, and oh my, how good this feels.

# A Two-Way Street

*I'm sixty-two years old and I've lived all my life in Manhattan. I'm a high school graduate; I didn't go to college because I was a dancer. I married very young, and after ten years, I had three children. I was married twenty-nine years and divorced about fourteen years ago. I am now in business for myself and am doing very well.*

I don't have a specific memory of Vicky telling me she was a lesbian; I think she must have told me bit by bit. She had been living with one young man for about eight years, and after she broke up with him, she went to San Francisco with another man. As I became aware of her seeing a woman, I remember thinking lesbianism was merely a phase. I also thought she was probably bisexual, and whether or not that is true I still don't know.

I went through a long period of time trying to understand why Vicky is a lesbian. I wondered whether the contributing factors were parental. I think they are—she doesn't—but it doesn't matter. One is what one is, yet Vicky and I do have different opinions on this. She has said that by taking on the question of who "caused" her lesbianism—her father or myself—we are taking over her life and her choice. She feels she is very much her own person and not just someone's daughter. My ex-husband does not accept her lifestyle; this has caused her a great deal of pain, and me a huge amount of anger. His attitude is totally unforgivable.

I don't go around with a placard saying my daughter is a lesbian. I feel that it is a personal aspect of life. If she was living with a boy named Don, I wouldn't wear that on a placard either, it's a personal thing. I find that when talking about her with friends and acquaintances, it's much more interesting to talk about what she is doing than who she is sleeping with. Those are the things you say about people you care about; what they do, what they accomplish, how they live their lives. My close friends know about her, some are accepting and some have offered their "condolences." Casual business friends certainly do not know about her lesbianism, as they don't know such personal information about any of my children. I talk about all three of my kids through talking about what they do. I did find out that my niece, who lives near Vicky, is also a lesbian. I mentioned it to my brother on the phone one day, casually saying that I thought it funny that both our oldest girls were lesbians. He giggled, said something brief and let it drop. I called my niece to tell her I may have slipped something I shouldn't have, and she said he hadn't been able to acknowledge her being a lesbian and that was the first time he had ever admitted it.

Going to visit Vicky is always a great personal experience for me. I visit her and her friends, and they are always so warm, and so accepting of me. To an outsider, the San Francisco lesbian community seems to be very supportive and accepting. Whatever Vicky is doing, I go along with her, to activities, community events, and to meet and visit with her friends. One close friend of hers called me while I was out there and asked me over to dinner on a night Vicky was busy. And this year, two different women whom I had met through Vicky in San Francisco visited me when they came to New York. We went swimming, had dinner together, and I really enjoyed spending time with these women.

In contrast, I am no longer part of my two sons' lives. There is a love relationship between us, but not a close relationship. I am not included in their lives as I am when I visit Vicky. I become part of her life; it's such a great experience. She tells her friends her mother is coming, and it's a positive thing—and not something said with a groan. Her friends are aware that I am straight, come from a straight society, and lead a straight life. Nevertheless, I am given so much warmth and acceptance from them. It's been really great for me and I am very grateful for all of it. I believe that lesbianism is not only something that is happening to our daughters, but creates an experience that can be very positive to us as parents. It's wonderful to realize that all the support and acceptance I have received is coming from people who are looking for acceptance, been denied acceptance and yet are so generous in their acceptance of me.

This is something for other mothers to think about; not only what they can do for their daughters, but what their daughters can do for them. If we reach out to our daughters we can gain so much support and understanding. I visit Vicky many times each year and am continually looking for excuses to visit more!

JUANITA RIOS

# Here, and There

I have a daughter, Mary, whom I adopted at three months old, and she is a lesbian. She was a difficult child, and a tomboy, and now I see the reason for it. It's a tragic story.

My daughter was very affected by my divorce which happened when she was eleven. She was raised in Monterey, where everything was so proper; the whole social scene was so strict, so affluent and professional. With the breaking up of the family, she just went berserk. She rebelled, and though she was very smart, quit school, and just ran around. Unfortunately she got involved with people who are irresponsible, and to this day—she'll be twenty-seven this year—she's been in and out of jail. It's a very sad thing for me, and I know a lot of it has to do with being so confused and feeling unaccepted. At the time, I didn't know what the problem was.

After the divorce, she went with her father, who would let her do whatever she wanted. She was away from me until two years ago, when she said she wanted to live with me. In the meantime, she was in and out of the juvenile halls.

When I came back to San Francisco four years ago, I realized I had to get myself informed about homosexuality. I am a Catholic, a strict Catholic. I live by the rules, but I don't want to be narrow-minded. I saw a *Dear Abby* column about homosexuality and wrote away for the name and number of a woman in the Parents and Friends of Lesbians and Gays group there in the city. She was fantas-

*My mother and father were from Nicaragua, and I was born in this country but raised in their culture. I grew up here in San Francisco's Mission District and later went to college in Berkeley. I married and lived for twenty years in Monterey, California where I adopted two children. I also lived in Acapulco for five years. I now teach bilingual adult education in a local community college.*

tic and I went to the meetings and just loved them.

Mary spent six months with me a couple of years ago after getting out of jail. She got a good job, went to some of the parents' meetings with me, and that beautiful woman inside of her surfaced—for the first time. But she was also in love with a woman who was a drug addict, who had a child, and Mary spent a lot of time writing her and thinking about her. I knew something was still wrong. After six months, she violated her parole, went back to her lover, and ended up back in jail. Last year, she came for a month, but she went on welfare, was out every night, and then her girlfriend came here and stayed. My mother was also here and it was a nightmare. I finally told Mary and her girlfriend to get out. Her whole attitude was very criminal and I was afraid. She and this woman left, and I haven't seen her since.

Mary's problem is not that she is a lesbian, it's more of a social problem. But it all triggers from the very beginning of her sexual identity; she just unfortunately tried to escape and not cope with it all. She has been on drugs throughout this time and I am afraid her mind has been affected. It's such a tragic story. My ex-husband recently told me that a friend of hers called to let us know Mary wanted us to know she was okay. At least she is alive.

I don't understand homosexuality. All I am convinced is that it is something you don't choose. I know that. When I first wanted to educate myself about homosexuality, I went to a Catholic priest. He gave me the okay to go to the parents' group. I don't understand it. It's a mystery, but if God made a group of people this way, they must be that way. To ask Mary to be different would be like asking me to be different—that's a really sound feeling I have about it.

This was confirmed over and over again as I met other homosexuals. I had not known others except my daughter. It was wonderful to meet other young gay people, and older gay people, too. I think it's a lack of knowledge and education that makes people feel so negative, but it's such a struggle because it's so contrary to what society believes. I don't understand it, but I certainly can't condemn it. I just hope and pray my daughter will find her way. She knows I love her and accept her as she is, but it's very painful. I haven't gone off the deep end because I have great faith. I cannot lose hope. So many parents don't want to face the situation. They try to deny it or live in another world. I meet so many young people who tell us in the parents' group that they wish their parents would accept them. They are so afraid of rejection. I just cannot understand how a parent can turn away from a child. I just cannot understand that. They should be able to love them more knowing that they have a rougher way in life.

I met a young man from Costa Rica at the group, and when I was in Costa Rica, I went to see his parents. His mother, who was very religious, refused to accept him. I told her I had a lesbian daughter. She said that he could change, that she absolutely would not accept his homosexuality, but that she accepted him. She said God would change him! It was not a very pleasant situation for either of us.

A few years ago, I established a program for mid-life Hispanic women, including education and job options. I was dealing with one woman whose son I had met briefly. I told her I was involved with the parents' group, I thought her son was gay, and that her reaction to my involvement in the group made me suspect it. I called the son to make sure I was on target, and sure enough I was. So I asked her if she wanted to go to a meeting with me, and she cried, she had no one to turn to. She had never talked of it and was afraid to let anyone know. She was really hurting. So she went to the meeting and has grown so much in the last two years it's incredible. She is going back to San Salvador soon and is going to tell her sister. Her son was worried about not being accepted by his aunt. She told him, "It doesn't matter, your mother accepts you." It's amazing how she has changed in such a short time.

I haven't done a lot, but I feel good about having touched a life here and there.

ERIN FINDLAY

## "Girlfriends!"

I'm fifty-seven and live in Northern California. I work at Girlfriends, a lesbian magazine edited by my daughter. Girlfriends covers lesbians in the arts, philosophies of lesbian life, and lesbian sexuality, including photographs.

I am a widow, so when my daughter came out, I was on my own. Trained as an academic, Heather was going to be a professor but could not find work. Though she interviewed for many jobs, she was tremendously disappointed when she was not chosen. I think the difficulty of her finding work had to do with her being an out lesbian. I think there are these old guys in academia who just don't want someone like her around.

Heather looked for other work and landed a job at a lesbian magazine. She showed me the magazine, and I thought it was very explicit and pornographic. It even included photos of naked women, but after a while I developed a veneer and stopped being shocked by them. One time I set her up with a friend's Cadillac for a prop at a nude photo shoot. My pal and I acted like police and kept the public away during the shoot. I felt very pioneering!

Eventually Heather got more frustrated at that job and announced she was going to resign and start a new magazine. She asked me what I thought of the name *Girlfriends* for her new endeavor. She also asked me to support her financially with the project and help out with the business side of things. I was offered the title of publisher. This was a big decision for me. I had just been widowed and was playing tennis and bridge, doing some volunteer work, but not doing anything very productive. Heather's request came at a good time. I got myself a computer and learned bookkeeping. The job became very full-time, and now I'm in charge of production and bookkeeping at *Girlfriends* magazine.

It's enlightening to work at a lesbian magazine. I'm learning about everything from lesbian mothering to stone butches (women who don't let other women make love to them). Heather is always giving me something to read.

I love our magazine. Though it includes nudity, I think the pictures are more arty than pornographic. I just don't see anything sleazy about it. Heather wants to celebrate lesbian sexuality and I think she is doing that in a nice way.

My friends have been supportive of me, and the people at my church know I'm a mother of a lesbian. I am Presbyterian and my church has been debating about whether to include lesbians and gay men. At a meeting called to discuss these issues, I talked about my daughter and I brought one of our magazines. Several people were absolutely shocked because of the nudity. I was taken aback by their responses because, by this time, I did not see anything wrong with nudity. I explained that the magazine is not for everybody, not even for every lesbian. But I also said that I didn't think we should be ashamed of our bodies or our sexual activities. Some people supported me, some didn't. Many people in the church still believe being gay or lesbian is immoral.

Heather was about twenty-one when she told me she was a lesbian. Like many mothers, my first feelings were those of guilt. I thought I had done something wrong raising her. She assured me I had not. Next, I felt regret. I was hoping to be a grandmother. Knowing absolutely nothing about homosexuality, I did not consider that she could have children. Finally, I was afraid of the uphill battle she would have to wage for the rest of her life. Unless things dramatically changed, she would always feel prejudice and maybe even be harmed physically for just being who she was.

Knowing Heather and her friends has been a tremendous learning experience. It's amazing how ordinary her friends are, not much different than my other daughter's friends. We have a lesbian couple in our office who are essentially man and wife. I watch them interact in the same way a heterosexual couple would.

With some women, you can tell they are lesbians, especially with butch women. Heather has a friend who she has been going with for five or six years. Sue is very butch and I have to admit that was a bit difficult at first. It was awkward going out to dinner at the yacht club; Sue has a short butch haircut and wears men's clothes. But now I like to think of her as part of my life. After all, she loves Heather and what is important is that your child is loved by her companion.

On Gay Pride Day, Heather and I marched in a parade together with a group of supportive parents. I carried a sign that said *Proud mom of a dyke.* Heather held a sign that said *Proud daughter of a cool mom.* I passed so many young women and men who were crying because they didn't get this kind of support from their parents. I couldn't imagine a mom who couldn't accept her daughter because she is a lesbian.

I am thankful that Heather has given me this opportunity to work with her. Not many women would want to work with their mother, especially on a lesbian magazine.

DIANE RAE

# Taming the Devils Within

*I'm a forty-nine-year-old Jewish woman, born and raised in Chicago. My parents were born in this country, and my grandparents came from Russia/Poland and Alsace-Lorraine. I've been divorced for eight years and am a realtor in Scottsdale, Arizona. We have no religious affiliations currently—religion was never on our list of priorities. Both my daughters are college graduates. I wish I were as well!*

My daughter's pronouncement, when she was twenty-two and in college, was the culmination of years of disquieting, unspoken dread. There were no specific reasons why I began to suspect her homosexuality from a very early age, but I did, as early as when she was six or seven. These thoughts were not actually at a conscious level, but whenever they started to surface I felt threatened and quickly suppressed them. I would start to concentrate on how pretty she was, how feminine and attractive, albeit she was a "tomboy" and loved to play ball with the boys. She was much less passive physically than girls tend to be, and we were proud of her athletic prowess and achievements.

During her growing years before high school, her closest friends were usually boys and she had great difficulties making girlfriends. She felt an indefinable hostility from them, and she became lonely and self-conscious. She used to cry and ask why she was "different" than the other girls. I remember a particularly poignant time when she and I were having one of our soul-searching talks and she said, "It seems I have to be someone different for every girl I'm with…I don't know what they want me to be, but I feel like I have to be what they want me to be. It's making me so tired." She was only about twelve or thirteen at the time.

In high school, she began to meet new people and

formed some friendships that have lasted through to the present. They were very intense and so infused with a quality of desperation that my suspicions overcame my reticence and I hesitantly and clumsily asked her if she perhaps ever had "unusual sexual fantasies or thoughts" that were bothering her. Her response was to laugh it off as an absurdity, which I found very reassuring.

For three more years, I ignored my own inner voices while she continued to date boys on an occasional basis, and partied a lot with her girlfriends. The summer she graduated from high school she came to me one night, and in a rather controlled panic, poured out a confession to having had a homosexual affair during spring break with a good friend's older, married sister. She was frightened and needed reassurance—and so did I! But my main concern was that she not judge herself too harshly and do something rash such as attempt suicide. So I tried to convey my love, and to suggest that she was young and experimenting sexually—a natural thing to do.

Another three years or so passed, and then one night, she called long distance from college and dropped it on me like a ton of weight. She was gay, she was sure of it, she had accepted it, and so must I. She also insisted there was no reason for me to feel guilty, or to try and lay blame anywhere. But of course, I knew otherwise! I could recite a whole litany of things my ex-husband and I had done wrong. Then I cried for having made her life more difficult, for the grandchildren she would never give me, for my imagined humiliation before family and friends.

Luckily, my mourning period was short-lived. I began to read up on homosexuality. I called a psychiatrist friend and discovered most of my fears were selfish and unfounded. Mainly, I quickly understood that she needed my love and support more than ever before, and that she was still the same person I'd loved before. She was not suicidal, promiscuous or sick. I realized how hard it was for her to face her own truth and how lucky I was that she trusted me enough to confide in me, despite the possibility of rejection.

Each mother who has had to come to terms with her daughter's lesbianism probably feels, as I did, that her situation is somehow different...that her problems are special. There are parts of each story that are unique. In my case, I blamed my behavior during my daughter's formative years— between two and five—the time after her sister was born. I was troubled and immature, and a potentially abusive parent, and I resorted to spanking her too frequently. Luckily, I got help through psychotherapy and that bomb was diffused quickly, but I always carried with me the guilt of those early years. My sixth sense was constantly watching for signs that I had sown the seeds of her problems by my own mistakes. Her admission was the confirmation of this fear.

I now believe the homosexual dynamics are probably a natural process occurring before birth, and that she would be a lesbian in spite of my actions, but every now and then that ogre raises its ugly head and gives me a moment's pause.

She has come out at work, with old friends, and now, with her father, my sister and nieces. The only two people she has intentionally not told are my parents, whom she loves dearly and thinks would be painfully confused about her lesbianism. She believes that they already sense it, but if they wanted to cope with it on a conscious level that they would ask why their lovely twenty-eight-year-old grand-daughter never dates men.

Her younger sister was not really surprised, nor upset, although for a few years, she thought the gay lifestyle was weird and strange. Her judgment has mellowed with time. They are closer than ever before and have even bought a home together as neither has a permanent relationship with anyone special at this time.

My primary personal devils to contend with and over-come were based upon the misinformation and mythology that abounds about gay children, which leads to guilt feelings and defensiveness. She came to that bridge and crossed it by herself, before helping me to the other side. She pressured me into seeking out some kind of group to share my doubts and fears with, and by a sheer stroke of dumb luck, I discovered Parents and Friends of Lesbians and Gays. It only took one meeting for me to regain a healthy perspective about myself as a mother of a gay daughter. I wish all parents could stop torturing themselves—as I did—with self-recriminations that only serve to widen the distance between them and their children.

MARGARET SMITH

# Finding My Way Through the Woods

*I feel blessed to have had two caring parents, a comfortable childhood, an excellent education, good health, a loving husband, three talented children, and now five beautiful grandchildren. I've been a social planner and administrator, a psychotherapist, and a volunteer rabble-rouser active in both the civil rights and gay rights movements. I love music, the out-of-doors, friends and books.*

Rachel came out to us after her freshman year at college. As I remember, it was something like the proverbial "Guess what, Mom—I'm a lesbian!" Like many parents, we were taken completely by surprise, but managed to say a few right things like "We love you, we want you to be happy, and everything will work out okay." What we thought privately was "Maybe it's just a phase, maybe she was seduced, what did I do wrong (working mothers are vulnerable to that one), maybe I should have stayed home more." We worried that she would have no one to take care of her, that we would not have grandchildren from her, that she would miss the joys of motherhood, that she might be harassed or worse.

As a Unitarian and a social worker, my head told me that homosexuality was perfectly normal and acceptable. But I felt as though something had kicked me in the gut. When I turned in desperation to my husband and asked what he thought, he answered with his typically brief but right-on response. "She's still our daughter, we love her and we can't change her. What is there to talk about?"

I now know that all our reactions were quite typical. Some parents go through them quickly while others suffer agony for years adjusting to a child's gayness. When children come out of the closet, the parents often go in. And parents' closets are often deeper, darker and longer than the child's. In our case, our reaction was relatively mild, but it took us ten years to feel comfortable enough with Rachel's orientation to talk freely about it.

Rachel was always a fairly quiet child, perhaps partly from being the middle child in a competitive threesome. She made good friends and stuck with them. Two out-of-town moves were very painful for her, disrupting school, neighborhood and friendships. She had been ill as an infant, hospitalized at twelve months for three days and I was not allowed to stay with her. When she came home, she clung to me like glue and has, perhaps, long struggled to overcome those early abandonment scars.

Rachel is a violinist, teaches, plays in various ensembles, has published a book on women composers, and truly enjoys her music—as we do, also. At age thirty, she found a partner, much to my relief and joy. She and Michelle seemed to have a mutually respectful, egalitarian relationship. They bought a home and appeared settled for life.

Sometimes when we visited Rachel, she would invite folks over or throw a party. We always enjoyed meeting her wonderful friends, who seemed consistently loving, bright-eyed and truly interesting people. What I both loved to hear, and was saddened to hear, was that her friends would say to her, "Gee, I wish my parents were as understanding as yours" or "I wish I could introduce my friends to my parents."

After early retirement from my work as a psychotherapist in a county mental health clinic and a move to the Blue Ridge Mountains, I started teaching workshops at the Women's Center of a local college. In searching for new topics to present, I suggested a seminar for families of gays. This was approved, I read up a storm, over-prepared and eight brave souls turned out. But they didn't want to hear my lecture; they wanted to talk with each other! Out of that grew what is now our local chapter of Parents, Families and Friends of Lesbians and Gays.

For the past two years, I have been a Regional Director of

PFLAG, interfacing with members in a four-state area, providing support for chapters and helping to organize new groups. Never have I met so many wonderful people, both straight and gay, and felt so quickly a kindred spirit with so many. I love helping other parents travel more quickly the same road we came so slowly. I feel privileged to share their journey.

My style is to pick a new topic every few years, read widely, and find ways to share this information with others. Last year, I chose bisexuality. I learned much about this "closet within the closet," something about the myths surrounding bisexuality, and even that many gays are prejudiced toward bi's, accusing them of being "only half-way out." As sex-researcher Kinsey taught, I now believe that sexual orientation, like many things, is more of a continuum than an either/or reality. It is typical of our culture to force us to take a side. While bi's may have a wider choice of partners, like all of us, I believe their orientation is largely a given at birth, except that it is somewhere in the "middle." I told my friends that next year I would be studying transsexuality.

Little did I guess! Rachel has recently informed us that she now realizes she is a transsexual. As far back as age ten, she has thought that she is really "a guy—a female guy"—a man in a woman's body. For some years, she felt that this was just part of being a lesbian, but she now realizes most lesbians, not only don't feel that way, they look down on those feelings. I've had a hard time accepting this as part of her reality because she has never been athletic, and certainly not particularly "butch." I have always considered her to be very pretty.

She has broken up with her partner, joined a support group for transsexuals, is in therapy and is struggling to decide whether she will undergo the arduous physical transition—a terribly tough decision.

At first I again thought—hoped—that this was a passing phase and even if it were real, that perhaps she could bury these feelings and go on living a woman's life. She did not want to see us or talk on the phone; she was not ready to answer my millions of questions and wanted "space." I feared I would never see my lovely daughter again, as such.

Unfortunately, Rachel's dilemma surfaced at the same time our son was undergoing intensive chemotherapy for acute myelogenous leukemia. I spent many weeks in long hospital visits and lending his gallant wife a hand with their three lively small children. I will join him again for an arduous stem cell transplant. We are impressed with Dean and Pat's plucky handling of this life-threatening illness. We are also heartened by our daughter, Stacy, a happily married Ph.D. engineer with two handsome young sons, and her caring support during this difficult summer. Both siblings were accepting of Rachel as a lesbian and continue to be understanding of her current dilemma. But we have all agreed we are not ready to share this with the extended family.

My husband has again expressed his brief "bottom line" to Rachel, "We love you no matter what, we want only your happiness." He was very close to her and I hurt more guessing his unexpressed feelings.

With two adult children in major life struggles, I felt emotionally drained. My grief and worry turned into a brief depression. Then my typical defensive reaction set in and I began to read everything available. I am beginning to dimly understand the transsexual's terrible dilemma.

First I had to learn to separate the many aspects of our sexuality. There is one's physical sex (male or female bodies), orientation (who turns us "on" as a sexual partner), sexual role (society's prescriptions for how boys and girls, men and women should behave), and gender (how we perceive ourselves, inside our skin). When all of these are synchronized, we are comfortable with the body and social roles given at birth. I learned, too, that there are more than two variations, if not a full continuum, for each of these aspects of our sexuality. Certainly we know that girls range in roles from very feminine to very tomboyish and boys likewise.

So now I had to add another dimension to the puzzle—that of gender identity. Some transgendered persons like to crossdress, lead a dual life, or, if they feel strongly, make an actual sex change. For my beloved Rachel, like many others, her self-concept just doesn't fit her body.

I have also been learning about the process transsexuals may undergo to change their bodies, including hormone therapy, extensive electrolysis (for male to female transitions), and then a series of surgeries—a long, arduous, risky, expensive and very awkward process. The end result is a compromise, at best.

What parent can easily see a child undergo all this? And not know what or who will emerge on the other side, whether s/he will find a special, understanding and loving partner, whether the career will survive, whether there will be happiness at the end of the trail?

In addition, my daughter has asked if we could now be "friends" and if she may call me "Margaret." In a vulnerable time, I felt rejected in my life's most important work, that of mother. While I was rethinking my role, I went through a period of calling her Rachel/Joshua and signing my name Mom/Margaret. Now we've made a deal—I call her Joshua (her chosen name) and she calls me Mom. (Oops, I mean "he." Changing pronouns is harder than the new name!)

We've discovered the benefits of e-mail and are writing almost daily. There is so much to "talk" about; I feel closer to him now. One thing I know for sure—I love him ever so much, I honor him for his brave honesty, and somehow, again, it will all work out.

I have many metaphors for this thing called "life"—a journey, a box of chocolates a la Forrest Gump, a growth process, learning to live with the unknown. Another metaphor is the path I am cutting through several acres of hilly forest behind our home. Exercise is always a good anti-dote for worry and I am healing from the summer's demands as I move logs, rake matted leaves and find my way through our beautiful wild woods.

# Purple Balloons on Market Street

About noon on June 26, 1983, my husband and I received a standing ovation from a cheering crowd of a quarter of a million. Men and women ran out from the sidelines of the crowd to embrace us and to thank us. The air was full of balloons, marching-band music, exuberant joy, and overwhelming love, much of it directed toward Bob and me. Yet only a dozen or so in the crowd knew our names. And it was hardly the kind of success story I could have written about to my college-class secretary to put in the alumnae notes.

*I was born to medical missionary parents in Istanbul, Turkey, where I lived at various periods of my life, and where I met my husband. I went to Wellesley College, and much later, to the University of California at Berkeley for a Master of Arts degree in Near Eastern Studies and a Master of Library Science degree. Since 1978, I have worked as a fundraiser with the American Friends Service Committee in San Francisco.*

Twenty-five years ago, I did write to the class secretary, proudly asking her to announce the birth of our first child, Margarett. I wanted all my classmates to share my joy. I dreamed that she would grow up bright, good, successful, go to college, marry an equally good, bright, and successful man, and have children.

This was the pattern in the family where I was the youngest of five, and I assumed it was the only pattern of fulfillment for a woman. But the intervening quarter-century has taught me a rich diversity of patterns and Margarett has been one of my principal instructors.

The June twenty-sixth extravaganza was, in fact, a celebration of our pride in Margarett, as Bob and I walked in the San Francisco Lesbian and Gay Freedom Day parade along with ten other middle-aged men and women under a banner that read *Parents and Friends of Lesbians and Gays*. I wasn't prepared for the crowd's enthusiasm. At first, it made me quite shy. Then of course, I began to enjoy the applause. And finally, I was deeply moved that parents publicly demonstrating their love for their homosexual children were, to the gay men and lesbians in that vast crowd, cause for cheering, clapping, and often tearful gratitude.

We wished Margarett and her lover Helen could have been there with us. But they live in New York City and were participating in the Freedom Day parade there.

I shall never forget the summer of 1976, the year Margarett graduated from high school. Our family was attending a church conference and one hot afternoon, Margarett plopped down beside me on the sleeping bag where I was resting, and after a long pause said, "Mom, have you noticed that I'm not around when there is a lesbian interest group scheduled?"

It was my turn to be quiet for a long time. I'd been picking up hints from friends of Margarett's that her relations with some girls were more than casual. One classmate had said something about "Margarett and the other dykes." And the mother of another had said of Margarett's high school that it was a difficult place for lesbians.

During her last two high school years, some of Margarett's attitudes and actions had puzzled Bob and me— having her head shaved, for example; getting a turkey tattooed on her shoulder; not wanting to spend more than thirty-six hours at home during vacation. I'd tried to accept that her restlessness was normal adolescent development, but in a family that prizes honesty and closeness, it troubled me. When the references to homosexuality began to be unmistakable, I decided to ask her outright. Her confession in the form of that question saved my asking.

My initial worry was that Margarett would wish that she were a boy. So I asked her if she was happy about being a lesbian and if she was glad to have a woman's body. She looked at me with such directness and answered *yes* with such conviction that I was reassured on that score.

For at least two more years, though, I found myself wondering if she should have psychiatric counseling, or if we should, and if there had been serious mistakes in the way we had brought her up. I wondered if she had had some traumatic, scarring experience with a man. Or been seduced by an older woman. Or gotten stuck in a pre-adolescent crush phase.

I was worried about the effect on our younger children. In a conversation with Margarett and Chris, who was the first woman to stay overnight in our house after Margarett had "come out," I begged them to be discreet, especially in front of Margarett's little sister, Catherine, who was then fifteen. I'm not sure what it was I feared, that she'd "catch lesbianism," that she'd ask me questions I couldn't answer, or what. Maybe I just wanted them to be so discreet that none of us would have to acknowledge what we had been told and could go on pretending that nothing had changed. Anyway, Margarett pointed out to me that months before she'd dared tell Bob and me, she'd told her brother and sister her "secret." I was left with my own discomfort and no younger children to "protect."

In my early discomfort, I didn't know anyone I could talk to. Mostly Bob and I avoided the subject. We didn't know how to talk about it to each other or even how to think about it ourselves. Bob now says that he used to have the standard American male prejudices against homosexuality. And we didn't know any other parents in our circumstances, or thought we didn't.

I resorted to reading, and unfortunately I was too shy, or too ashamed, to ask for guidance in my choice of books. I should have asked Margarett. She would probably have been pleased at my interest in becoming better informed, and she would surely have given me good recommendations. As it was, I tried to find what I could, and I looked in the wrong places.

In a religious bookstore, I found a book written by a woman psychiatrist. Here, I thought, would be the ultimate authority. That was five years after Margarett had told us about her lesbianism. She was already living in New York, supporting herself as a printer. I was on my way to visit her for the first time, and I'd taken the book along to read on the plane. This particular psychiatrist's thesis was that lesbians are endlessly searching for the love their mothers denied them in infancy. I was stricken! I began to sob so copiously that the passenger next to me asked me if something was wrong.

What could I say? "Yes, I've just found out that I've done something awful to my daughter." "No, no. I always cry over novels."

Behind my fear of what I might have done to Margarett, there still lingered the prejudice that something is wrong with a person who is in love with someone of the same sex.

I continued to look for clues that would explain how my daughter could deviate so far from an established family pattern. I carefully reviewed Margarett's life up to that point. She was the first child, a treasured delight to Bob and me. Being the youngest in our respective families, we had several nieces and nephews each by the time we were married, and we both loved first the idea and then the fact of being parents. When Margarett was sixteen months old, Paul was born, and two and a half years later, Catherine. My attention, if not my love, had surely been diverted from Margarett at an early age. But this is true in every family, and not every oldest girl is a lesbian!

I looked at family pictures and studied Margarett as a baby and a little girl. I saw a child who was bright, alert, independent, somewhat competitive, funny, occasionally secretive. She had a firm mouth and an erect posture that said, "I know what I want and it would probably be a good idea not to interfere too much in my getting it."

She liked school and did very well. She was conscientious and determined, and as she went along, mastered several skills, mostly by teaching herself and practicing over and over until she was satisfied. Occasionally, she would ask for instruction, but only as much as she felt she needed. She taught herself to roller skate, then to ride a bicycle, spending hours and hours by herself until she'd become expert. I think that this self-instruction gave her confidence to realize that she could learn by herself whatever she needed to know.

I think it is fortunate that, being the innovative ground-breaker she is, Margarett has this confidence and independence. During the first couple of years that Bob and I knew of her lesbianism—that period of time when we feared that something was wrong with her—we might have tried to change a more malleable child. And we might have done her and ourselves great harm.

I finally realized that searching for explanations for what made Margarett a lesbian was getting me nowhere. When I stopped looking for an answer in the past, within myself, and in books, and started looking, really looking at who Margarett is, I saw a young woman with whom I could find little fault.

She is not sick. Neither physically nor psychologically nor morally. She is competent, mature, confident, considerate, and most of the time, happy. She has the spare, strong build of a gymnast, a terrific sense of humor (no one can make me giggle as she does), a fiery sense of justice, good mechanical skills, and an intelligent curiosity that keeps her reading and learning though her formal education stopped after high school.

Margarett and Helen have lived together for six years. They have transformed the apartments (two, now) that they could afford from filthy, dingy New York tenements to cheerful, comfortable homes.

How to tell the extended family about Margarett's lesbianism has been tricky. I wanted them to know her as a complete person before knowing just this one aspect of her life. One of the last to know was my ninety-year-old mother. One day last summer, I visited her and took her for a drive. As we drove along, Mother asked, "Do Margarett or Catherine have boyfriends?"

I decided to plunge in. Mother had met Helen earlier that summer when the girls and I had stopped by at her nursing home. When she met Helen she said, "And this is Margarett's Helen!" So I thought it was going to be easy. But Mother didn't know, or had forgotten the vocabulary. Words like *lesbian* and *homosexual* she said she didn't understand. Finally I said, "Mother, Margarett and Helen live together as a couple. They give one another the same kind of love and support that a married couple do." And Mother said, "Ah, that I can understand!" Mother had, in a few moments, made the leap that took Bob and me two or three years.

For us, it wasn't a leap but a gradual process of understanding, appreciation, and acceptance. And now we've stopped looking for explanations, realizing at last what caused Margarett to be homosexual is unknown and probably unknowable. It is as irrelevant as what caused Paul to be left-handed, Catherine to have freckles, or, for that matter, her parents to be heterosexual.

While Bob, as I said, acknowledges that he used to have the traditional American male prejudice against "queers," he became active in supporting gay rights long before I did. In 1978, voters in California were asked to vote for the Briggs Initiative, which would have barred from the classroom any teacher who was homosexual or advocated gay rights. Bob, a public school teacher who was active in the civil rights movement and in the peace movement during the Vietnam War, hit the streets again, marching with Margarett in Sacramento to protest the initiative. Later that summer, he walked in the Gay Freedom Day parade.

Thanks to the hard work of many volunteers and the

innate good sense of the California electorate—at that time at any rate—the Briggs Initiative was defeated. Bob hasn't missed a Gay Freedom Day parade since.

Bob and I have become increasingly aware of the extent to which homosexual men and women have been oppressed. Margarett often wears a pin with a pink triangle on a gray circle. I had thought of it as merely an attractive design until she told me that it was the emblem homosexuals were forced to wear in Nazi Germany, just as Jews had to wear a yellow Star of David. I learned that the jocular-sounding term *fag* or *faggot* is not so funny when one realizes its origins—homosexuals burned at the stake in the Middle Ages. In fact, the language and humor of homophobia, like any ethnic slur, cease to be acceptable when one has felt their impact and pain.

When Bob and I realized that many gay men and lesbians we know are not able to talk to their parents about something so central in their lives as the person with whom they are in love, and that many parents are in deep personal anguish over having a homosexual child, we decided to do what we could in our community.

We discovered Parents and Friends of Lesbians and Gays and located the group in our area. We organized meetings in our own community. The structure is informal and we are listed with the local Gay Information Switchboard so other parents can find us. A nearby Lutheran church has offered us the use of their facilities. Often young gay men and lesbians come to meetings to be with accepting adults. They are very helpful to us parents who want and need further education.

A concern that often arises in the parents' group is the question of grandchildren. Interestingly enough, it is usually the fathers who feel most keenly the deprivation of not having grandchildren. Bob is no exception. He delighted in our children and is eager now for grandbabies. But Paul was married this summer and his wife has a five-year-old daughter. Bob and I are enjoying "instant" grandparent-hood. Moreover, we know three lesbian couples who have chosen to have children, so it is possible for parents of homosexual children to still be grandparents. Bob and I have also talked of taking in foster children after we retire. There are many ways to express the longing to enjoy small children.

A very positive development is that churches are beginning to recognize their obligation to counsel gays and their families, and to have support groups for them within the church. The religious community has a special responsibility, it seems to me, to consider the Biblical misinterpretation of homosexuality as "sin." My own religious conviction is to look to the inner dictates of the spirit for moral guidance. On the other hand, my upbringing and my early Bible study gave me a deep respect for the Bible. I find in Biblical teaching overwhelming persuasion on the side of love, tolerance, and affirmation of life. Jesus' harshest words are against hypocrisy. Paul's injunctions are against "unnatural" behavior. The Kinsey Institute's statistics of the 1950s show that ten percent of Americans are homosexual. That minority of us is part of nature and of its laws, too. Can we claim to love the Creator if we despise the creation? I'm not saying that every homosexual person is without sin. Rape, child molesting, sexual coercion of any kind is sinful. But the fact is that these aberrations are far more prevalent among heterosexual males than among homosexuals of either gender.

I have seen great improvement in the last few years in the attitude towards homosexuals, largely due to the efforts of brave men and women who write, sing, dance, and celebrate their experience for the better understanding of us all. I no longer have to confine my reading to books like the one that made me cry on the airplane. Most bookstores, and certainly all women's bookstores, have dozens of works by lesbian and gay authors who can teach us the positive, joyful, funny aspects of their lives: Rita Mae Brown, Adrienne Rich, Bar-

bara Deming, Sheila Ortiz Taylor, Harvey Fierstein, James Baldwin, and Christopher Isherwood, to mention only a few.

But there is still a long way to go until discrimination in jobs, housing, and child custody, is a thing of the past. There is a long way to go until the parents of homosexual children are free to love them completely without fear or shame. There is a long way to go before gay men and lesbians no longer think it's a big deal when ten parents march the length of Market Street in San Francisco as we did in the Freedom Day parade.

So while it was a heady experience for Bob and me to be the object of such love and gratitude, I look forward to the day when declaring our love for all our children will not be such a remarkable event.

## Some Facts to Consider

1. There is no one reason as to why, or how, people are or become lesbian, gay, bisexual—or heterosexual. Lesbians and gay men "come out" in many different ways and at many different points in their lives. Some of us come to understand our sexual orientation early in our lives. Others realize they are gay or lesbian during puberty. Still others come out later in life, sometimes after heterosexual relationships.

2. There are gays and lesbians in every cultural group, blacks, whites, Hispanics, etc. There are gays and lesbians living all over the world.

3. Surveys set the number of gays and lesbians to be approximately one in every ten people. Sexuality studies show that about one third of society has experienced some sort of same-sex encounter, but not all of these people identify as homosexual.

4. There are many different ways to be gay or lesbian just as there are many different ways of being straight. Many people are not exclusively straight or gay. Some people are bisexual and some people's sexual orientation shifts over time. There is no "cure" for homosexuality though some people claim this is possible.

## Parents and Friends of Lesbians and Gays

PFLAG is a non-profit federation active throughout the United States and in other countries. Most local PFLAG groups operate a hotline staffed by parents of gays and lesbians. A call to these groups will find a sympathetic and understanding listener, someone who has had a similar experience. Contacts for local groups and hotlines may be found in community newspapers, or by calling gay and lesbian switchboards. Often these numbers can be found in the white pages of the phone book.

In addition to organizing local drop-in support groups, PFLAG makes available publications and both audio and video tapes on different aspects of homosexuality. For a list of educational materials, send a self-addressed stamped envelope to the PFLAG headquarters. PFLAG can also furnish speakers for organizations and community groups.

For a contact in your area, write to: PFLAG, 1101 14th St. NW, Suite 1030, Washington DC, 20005. Phone: (202) 638-4200 Fax: (202) 638-0243 E-mail address: PFLAGntl@aol.com.


## Books and Other Resources

The number of good books for parents is constantly growing. Even the large chain bookstores now carry books about lesbians and gays. Libraries can also be a good resource, although not all libraries will stock books about homosexuality.

Aside from asking your daughter for suggestions on reading materials, talking to the staff at a gay and lesbian or alternative bookstore will help you find what you need. Lambda Rising, one of the country's largest outlets for gay and lesbians books and videos, operates a toll-free phone service staffed by knowledgeable booksellers. Lambda Rising will send books in plain brown wrappers anywhere in the country. Lambda Rising can be reached between 10 am and 12 pm Eastern Standard Time at 1-800-621-6969.

A Different Light Bookstore also offers nationwide mail order service. They can be reached at 1-800-343-4002 or (212) 989-4850.

## About the Editor

Louise Rafkin is a writer and editor living on Cape Cod, Massachusetts. She is the author of a number of books, for both children and adults, including *Different Mothers: Sons and Daughters of Lesbians Talk About Their Lives*. Her articles have appeared in the *New York Times*, the *Ladies Home Journal* and *Out* magazine among others.

# Books from Cleis Press

## Sexual Politics

*Forbidden Passages: Writings Banned in Canada* introductions by Pat Califia and Janine Fuller.
ISBN: 1-57344-020-5 24.95 cloth;
ISBN: 1-57344-019-1 14.95 paper.

*Good Sex: Real Stories from Real People,* second edition, by Julia Hutton.
ISBN: 1-57344-001-9 29.95 cloth;
ISBN: 1-57344-000-0 14.95 paper.

*The Good Vibrations Guide to Sex: How to Have Safe, Fun Sex in the '90s* by Cathy Winks and Anne Semans.
ISBN: 0-939416-83-2 29.95 cloth;
ISBN: 0-939416-84-0 16.95 paper.

*I Am My Own Woman: The Outlaw Life of Charlotte von Mahlsdorf* translated by Jean Hollander.
ISBN: 1-57344-011-6 24.95 cloth;
ISBN: 1-57344-010-8 12.95 paper.

*Madonnarama: Essays on Sex and Popular Culture* edited by Lisa Frank and Paul Smith.
ISBN: 0-939416-72-7 24.95 cloth;
ISBN: 0-939416-71-9 9.95 paper.

*Public Sex: The Culture of Radical Sex* by Pat Califia.
ISBN: 0-939416-88-3 29.95 cloth;
ISBN: 0-939416-89-1 12.95 paper.

*Sex Work: Writings by Women in the Sex Industry* edited by Frédérique Delacoste and Priscilla Alexander.
ISBN: 0-939416-10-7 24.95 cloth;
ISBN: 0-939416-11-5 16.95 paper.

*Susie Bright's Sexual Reality: A Virtual Sex World Reader* by Susie Bright.
ISBN: 0-939416-58-1 24.95 cloth;
ISBN: 0-939416-59-X 9.95 paper.

*Susie Bright's Sexwise* by Susie Bright.
ISBN: 1-57344-003-5 24.95 cloth;
ISBN: 1-57344-002-7 10.95 paper.

Susie Sexpert's Lesbian Sex World by Susie Bright.
ISBN: 0-939416-34-4 24.95 cloth;
ISBN: 0-939416-35-2 9.95 paper.

## Lesbian and Gay Studies

*Best Gay Erotica 1996* selected by Scott Heim, edited by Michael Ford.
ISBN: 1-57344-053-1 24.95 cloth;
ISBN: 1-57344-052-3 12.95 paper.

*Best Lesbian Erotica 1996* selected by Heather Lewis, edited by Tristan Taormino.
ISBN: 1-57344-055-8 24.95 cloth;
ISBN: 1-57344-054-X 12.95 paper.

*Boomer: Railroad Memoirs* by Linda Niemann.
ISBN: 0-939416-55-7 12.95 paper.

*The Case of the Good-For-Nothing Girlfriend* by Mabel Maney.
ISBN: 0-939416-90-5 24.95 cloth;
ISBN: 0-939416-91-3 10.95 paper.

*The Case of the Not-So-Nice Nurse* by Mabel Maney.
ISBN: 0-939416-75-1 24.95 cloth;
ISBN: 0-939416-76-X 9.95 paper.

*Dagger: On Butch Women* edited by Roxxie, Lily Burana, Linnea Due.
ISBN: 0-939416-81-6 29.95 cloth;
ISBN: 0-939416-82-4 14.95 paper.

*Dark Angels: Lesbian Vampire Stories* edited by Pam Keesey.
ISBN: 1-57344-015-9 24.95 cloth;
ISBN 1-7344-014-0 10.95 paper.

*Daughters of Darkness: Lesbian Vampire Stories* edited by Pam Keesey.
ISBN: 0-939416-77-8 24.95 cloth;
ISBN: 0-939416-78-6 9.95 paper.

*Different Daughters: A Book by Mothers of Lesbians,* second edition, edited by Louise Rafkin.
ISBN: 1-57344-051-5 24.95 cloth;
ISBN: 1-57344-050-7 12.95 paper.

*Different Mothers: Sons & Daughters of Lesbians Talk About Their Lives* edited by Louise Rafkin.
ISBN: 0-939416-40-9 24.95 cloth;
ISBN: 0-939416-41-7 9.95 paper.

*Dyke Strippers: Lesbian Cartoonists A to Z* edited by Roz Warren.
ISBN: 1-57344-009-4 29.95 cloth;
ISBN: 1-57344-008-6 16.95 paper.

*Girlfriend Number One: Lesbian Life in the '90s* edited by Robin Stevens.
ISBN: 0-939416-79-4 29.95 cloth;
ISBN: 0-939416-8 12.95 paper.

*Hothead Paisan: Homicidal Lesbian Terrorist* by Diane DiMassa.
ISBN: 0-939416-73-5 14.95 paper.

*A Lesbian Love Advisor* by Celeste West.
ISBN: 0-939416-27-1 24.95 cloth;
ISBN: 0-939416-26-3 9.95 paper.

*More Serious Pleasure: Lesbian Erotic Stories and Poetry* edited by the Sheba Collective.
ISBN: 0-939416-48-4 24.95 cloth;
ISBN: 0-939416-47-6 9.95 paper.

*Nancy Clue and the Hardly Boys in A Ghost in the Closet* by Mabel Maney.
ISBN: 1-57344-013-2 24.95 cloth;
ISBN: 1-57344-012-4 10.95 paper.

*The Night Audrey's Vibrator Spoke: A Stonewall Riots Collection* by Andrea Natalie.
ISBN: 0-939416-64-6 8.95 paper.

*Queer and Pleasant Danger: Writing Out My Life* by Louise Rafkin.
ISBN: 0-939416-60-3 24.95 cloth;
ISBN: 0-939416-61-1 9.95 paper.

*Revenge of Hothead Paisan: Homicidal Lesbian Terrorist* by Diane DiMassa.
ISBN: 1-57344-016-7 16.95 paper.

*Rubyfruit Mountain: A Stonewall Riots Collection* by Andrea Natalie.
ISBN: 0-939416-74-3 9.95 paper.

*Serious Pleasure: Lesbian Erotic Stories and Poetry* edited by the Sheba Collective.
ISBN: 0-939416-46-8 24.95 cloth;
ISBN: 0-939416-45-X 9.95 paper.

*Switch Hitters: Lesbians Write Gay Male Erotica and Gay Men Write Lesbian Erotica* edited by Carol Queen and Lawrence Schimel.
ISBN: 1-57344-022-1 24.95 cloth;
ISBN: 1-57344-021-3 12.95 paper.

## Politics of Health

*The Absence of the Dead Is Their Way of Appearing* by Mary Winfrey Trautmann.
ISBN: 0-939416-04-2 8.95 paper.

*Don't: A Woman's Word* by Elly Danica.
ISBN: 0-939416-23-9 21.95 cloth;
ISBN: 0-939416-22-0 8.95 paper

*1 in 3: Women with Cancer Confront an Epidemic* edited by Judith Brady.
ISBN: 0-939416-50-6 24.95 cloth;
ISBN: 0-939416-49-2 10.95 paper.

*Voices in the Night: Women Speaking About Incest* edited by Toni A.H. McNaron and Yarrow Morgan.
ISBN: 0-939416-02-6 9.95 paper.

*With the Power of Each Breath: A Disabled Women's Anthology* edited by Susan Browne, Debra Connors and Nanci Stern.
ISBN: 0-939416-09-3 24.95 cloth;
ISBN: 0-939416-06-9 10.95 paper.

*Woman-Centered Pregnancy and Birth* by the Federation of Feminist Women's Health Centers.
ISBN: 0-939416-03-4 11.95 paper.

## Reference

*Putting Out: The Essential Publishing Resource Guide For Gay and Lesbian Writers*, third edition, by Edisol W. Dotson.
ISBN: 0-939416-86-7 29.95 cloth;
ISBN: 0 939416-87-5 12.95 paper.

## Fiction

*Cosmopolis: Urban Stories by Women* edited by Ines Rieder.
ISBN: 0-939416-36-0 24.95 cloth;
ISBN: 0-939416-37-9 9.95 paper.

*Dirty Weekend: A Novel of Revenge* by Helen Zahavi.
ISBN: 0-939416-85-9 10.95 paper.

*A Forbidden Passion* by Cristina Peri Rossi.
ISBN: 0-939416-64-0 24.95 cloth;
ISBN: 0-939416-68-9 9.95 paper.

*Half a Revolution: Contemporary Fiction by Russian Women* edited by Masha Gessen.
ISBN 1-57344-007-8 $29.95 cloth;
ISBN 1 57344-006-X $12.95 paper.

*In the Garden of Dead Cars* by Sybil Claiborne.
ISBN: 0-939416-65-4 24.95 cloth;
ISBN: 0-939416-66-2 9.95 paper.

*Night Train To Mother* by Ronit Lentin.
ISBN: 0-939416-29-8 24.95 cloth;
ISBN: 0-939416-28-X 9.95 paper.

*The One You Call Sister: New Women's Fiction* edited by Paula Martinac.
ISBN: 0-939416-30-1 24.95 cloth;
ISBN: 0-939416031-X 9.95 paper.

*Only Lawyers Dancing* by Jan McKemmish.
ISBN: 0-939416-70-0 24.95 cloth;
ISBN: 0-939416-69-7 9.95 paper.

*Seeing Dell* by Carol Guess
ISBN: 1-57344-024-8 24.95 cloth;
ISBN: 1-57344-023-X 12.95 paper.

*Unholy Alliances: New Women's Fiction* edited by Louise Rafkin.
ISBN: 0-939416-14-X 21.95 cloth;
ISBN: 0-939416-15-8 9.95 paper.

*The Wall* by Marlen Haushofer.
ISBN: 0-939416-53-0 24.95 cloth;
ISBN: 0-939416-54-9 paper.

*We Came All The Way from Cuba So You Could Dress Like This?: Stories* by Achy Obejas.
ISBN: 0-939416-92-1 24.95 cloth;
ISBN: 0-939416-93-X 10.95 paper.

## Latin America

*Beyond the Border: A New Age in Latin American Women's Fiction* edited by Nora Erro-Peralta and Caridad Silva-Núñez.
ISBN: 0-939416-42-5 24.95 cloth;
ISBN: 0-939416-43-3 12.95 paper.

*The Little School: Tales of Disappearance and Survival in Argentina* by Alicia Partnoy.
ISBN: 0-939416-08-5 21.95 cloth;
ISBN: 0-939416-07-7 9.95 paper.

*Revenge of the Apple* by Alicia Partnoy.
ISBN: 0-939416-62-X 24.95 cloth;
ISBN: 0-939416-63-8 8.95 paper.

## Autobiography, Biography, Letters

*Peggy Deery: An Irish Family at War* by Nell McCafferty.
ISBN: 0-939416-38-7 24.95 cloth;
ISBN: 0-939416-39-5 9.95 paper.

*The Shape of Red: Insider/Outsider Reflections* by Ruth Hubbard and Margaret Randall.
ISBN: 0-939416-19-0 24.95 cloth;
ISBN: 0-939416-18-2 9.95 paper.

*Women & Honor: Some Notes on Lying* by Adrienne Rich.
ISBN: 0-939416-44-1 3.95 paper.

## Animal Rights

*And a Deer's Ear, Eagle's Song and Bear's Grace: Relationships Between Animals and Women* edited by Theresa Corrigan and Stephanie T. Hoppe.
ISBN: 0-939416-38-7 24.95 cloth;
ISBN: 0-939416-39-5 9.95 paper.

*With a Fly's Eye, Whale's Wit and Woman's Heart: Relationships Between Animals and Women* edited by Theresa Corrigan and Stephanie T. Hoppe.
ISBN: 0-939416-24-7 24.95 cloth;
ISBN: 0-939416-25-5 9.95 paper.

## *Ordering information*

Since 1980, Cleis Press has published progressive books by women. We welcome your order and will ship your books as quickly as possible. Individual orders must be prepaid (U.S. dollars only). Please add 15% shipping. PA residents add 6% sales tax. Mail orders: Cleis Press, PO Box 8933, Pittsburgh PA 15221. MasterCard and Visa orders: include account number, exp. date, and signature. FAX your credit card order: (412) 937-1567. Or, phone us Mon–Fri, 9 am–5 pm EST: (412) 937-1555.